CRITICAL ACCLAIM FOR

The Art of Leading Yourself

"As surely as there is a science of emotional intelligence, there is an art to it as well. This book contains such art. Informative, personal, inspirational and provocative, it is always readable; full of real life stories and events. Randi Noyes has helped many people get in touch with and find the courage and wisdom to know when to follow their feelings. The Art of Leading Yourself *provides an inspirational and entertaining view of emotional intelligence in action."*

— Dr. John D. Mayer, University of New Hampshire,
Originator of the first scientific definition of emotional intelligence

"No wonder The Art of Leading Yourself *became a bestseller! It is powerful, wise and potentially life changing. I strongly recommend it!"*

— Judy Peterson, Businesswoman, speaker, and author of
Something of Your Own and *Follow Your Heart*

"Significant for all who consider personal development paramount, including leaders in business and industry. It emphasizes that our existential challenge is to take responsibility for our own lives, for our major decisions, actions and failures. After reading the book, I gave it to my group's co-leader and suggested, 'Read it now!'"

— Leif J. Braaten, Ph.D.
Institute of Psychology, University of Oslo

"Randi's book is a great tool to make people more whole and more secure. It's fascinating reading!"

— Grete Roede, Chair, Grete Roede, A.S.,
Businesswoman of the Year, 1999

"*Randi's writing differs from typical management literature. She helps readers gain insight and increase emotional nearness and love for others. An important contribution to the art of living, this book can help people uncover their strengths and sense of purpose. I give it my highest recommendation.*"

— Judge Jens-Jacob Sander
County Court, Oslo, Norway

"*A very useful personal development tool. As Randi shows, a person is responsible for him/herself and is free to make choices. Here lies the key to the best possible life.*"

— Karl Moursund
President, Finansbanken, A.S.A.

"*My life and career were going uphill until, at age forty-three, I hit a wall. The practical tools in Randi Noyes' book have helped me to a richer and fuller life than I thought possible.*"

— Steinar Meylaender-Larsen,
President, Selvaag Bygg, A.S.

"*What Randi Noyes has developed is genius—and simple. It won't go out of style in three years; it works today and it will work in the future!*"

— Dr. Kjell Hultmann

"*The Art of Leading Yourself is a useful tool, helping everyone in our organization to move in the same direction. I have given the book to our store managers and to all our executives.*"

— Per-Martin Eng, President, Lindex AS

THE ART
of
LEADING YOURSELF

—◆—

Tap the Power of Your
Emotional Intelligence

RANDI B. NOYES

Vermilion
LONDON

1 3 5 7 9 10 8 6 4 2

First published in the US in 2001 by Cypress House
First published in the United Kingdom in 2003 by Vermilion, an imprint of
Ebury Press
Random House UK Ltd.
Random House
20 Vauxhall Bridge Road
London SW1V 2SA

Random House Australia (Pty) Limited
20 Alfred Street, Milsons Point, Sydney,
New South Wales 2061, Australia

Random House New Zealand Limited
18 Poland Road, Glenfield,
Auckland 10, New Zealand

Random House (Pty) Limited
Endulini, 5A Jubilee Road, Parktown 2193, South Africa

Random House UK Limited Reg. No. 954009
www.randomhouse.co.uk
Papers used by Vermilion are natural, recyclable products made from wood
grown in sustainable forests.

A CIP catalogue record is available for this book from the British Library.

ISBN: 0091889731

Printed and bound in Great Britain by
Mackays of Chatham plc, Chatham, Kent

"This above all, to thine own self be true;
And it must follow as the night the day,
Thou canst not then be false to any man."

— William Shakespeare *(Hamlet)*

FOREWORD

Randi's stated mission is "to bring out hidden resources in others and in myself in order to create the lives we want to live." She does this superbly, clearly explaining the information, providing real-life examples, and offering exercises so people can apply the principles to their own lives. She defines Emotional Intelligence and clarifies what it means in everyday living and how readers can increase it in themselves. The book also inspires by describing Randi's courage in understanding and taking charge of her own life and building her Emotional Intelligence before its importance became widely understood.

Randi is masterful at helping people understand themselves and become happier and more productive—a marvelous combination—by discovering and building on their strengths. As importantly, she teaches people how to get in touch with and understand the emotions that can get in their way, and how to channel the energy of these emotions in positive directions. The popularity of her book in Scandinavia demonstrates how she carried that mastery into writing to reach many individuals and groups. I'm delighted that it's now available in English to help many more. I strongly recommend this book for a deeper understanding of yourself and others, and for getting more of what you want in your life.

— LeRoy Malouf, Chairman, LMA, Inc.,
leadership consulting firm, USA

Acknowledgements

The author offers grateful thanks to:

Journalist Kristin Hetle, who helped create this book. Dearest Kristin, we dared to dream that the book would be of great value to people around the world. I can never thank you enough! It's amazing how much joy has come from our book. You're a great editor and writer and my dear friend. Thank you for all the hard work and the fun!

My publishers: Grøndal Dreyer, Energica, and Cypress House, USA, for believing in the book.

My first editor, Tove Gulbrandsen—you believed so deeply, knowing firsthand how important the book is to living a meaningful life. You're an inspiration.

Inger Husbo-Schoyen, for her invaluable advice.

Dr. John Mayer, whose research in emotional intelligence has been a great inspiration.

Judge Sander, who believed in the book, and Leif Braaten, professor of psychology at the University of Oslo, for being so excited about the book and recommending it to others.

Elizabeth Bailey, for her skilled treatment of the English language: you moved the book out of a true language mess. Thanks for being a friend in the process, and giving me courage to go on with the project.

My dear friend, Professor Alexander Pihl, who improved the manuscript: you helped me get the meaning across as only you could, and inspired me to make the book even better.

My lifelong friend Judy Peterson. We never stopped believing in following our hearts. My friend Maria Kalamaki, for believing in me and supporting my projects, and my great friend Inger Johanne Fuglesang for being my professional partner in leadership training for years. Without all the experience we shared there would have been no book. My dear friend, Liv Arnesen, who, by crossing the Antarctic on skis, inspired millions of us to dream.

Chris Casper, my friend of sixteen years, for teaming up with me to get our books out. We did it, Chris; it's time to celebrate!

Thank you to my dear mentor of twenty-one years, LeRoy Malouf, chairman of LMA, Inc. Where would I be without you? When the student was ready the teacher was there. You sent me to the best trainers and shared the most profound conversations for years and years. You put me on a road full of success and meaning! Thank you for all you've taught me, and for being my friend for life.

Joe Shaw, who made this book so easy to read and taught me that less is more. I want to thank Stina Smemo, Publicity Manager, for uncovering the book and bringing it to Random House and Amanda Hemmings, Editorial Director at Random House, for believing so much in my book.

I also want to thank Dr. Steven Covey for endorsing my book and ForeWord Magazine for giving it the silver award for "Book of the Year" in the category of business. I feel overwhelmed and deeply thankful to all.

Last but not least, my son Erik, for loving me unconditionally just as I am—the first person ever to do that. Without your love and support I wouldn't have dared grow to become all of me. Thank you for being true to your heart and for believing in yourself, my book, and me. I believe in you all the way!

Finally, my boyfriend/husband, the greatest gift in my midlife years. You've supported me in ways I never dared dream of. You're so real, so honest and so caring. Thank you for loving my book and me and being one of the very best leaders I know! Happy is the man or woman who has a great leader.

CONTENTS

4: Learning to Soar:
Exercises in Managing Your Feelings ---------- 119

5: Getting Unblocked:
Stories about Grownups ------------------------- 133

6: What to Do Next ------------------------------- 141

INTRODUCTION

More than 180,000 people have benefited from the book you're holding. Since its publication in 1995, I've received letters and phone calls every day from people who tell me how the book has made a difference, serving to inspire, to motivate, to challenge, and to change the way they think about their lives. It's been deeply moving to learn what an impact the book has had on individuals, couples and corporations. I'm grateful that I could provide a catalyst for helping people take charge of their lives.

Success with Meaning

I wrote this book for those who want to move their lives in a healthier, more rewarding direction; who want a better, richer and more meaningful life. This book is for people who want to give their all while here on Earth, who want to contribute creatively to the world around them. When we feel that life is very difficult, we ask how we can reshape our existence to make life what we always dreamed it could be. That's what this book is all about.

Life can be difficult now and then, don't let anyone convince you otherwise. Over the years, my experience, seminars and coaching have shown me that, deep down, people are very much alike. We all struggle with the same problems, albeit in different disguises, yet we deal with these similar problems in very different ways.

This book is about life as it really is, about who we are behind our masks. It's a book of hope, strength, and last but not least, love. It's meant to be a loving "friend" who talks directly to you and challenges you instead of simply agreeing with you. And I hope it provokes you from time to time, as a good friend often will.

Focus on Your Strengths

Unlike many books, this one doesn't try to change you. Instead, it asks you to look inside yourself and find the strength and talents you already possess—the things that will guide you to a happier, more fulfilled life. It asks you to be aware of yourself, to be aware of your feelings and to use them intelligently, and it demands that you embrace the person you are. In short, it builds on the foundation of your strengths and values; it doesn't require you to correct your weaknesses in order to be successful. Through self-awareness, self-management, self-acceptance and self-empowerment, this book will help you soar.

Emotional Intelligence (EI)

Many participants in my seminars question whether they are really intelligent enough to achieve the things they aspire to. I respond, "What is intelligence?" For decades, intelligence quotient (IQ) has been considered the most important measure of what a person is capable of. IQ, however, can only tell you how you compare to the average performance in abstract reasoning. Thanks to more recent research, we now know that emotional intelligence, or EI, is equally important.

In 1990, American psychologist Dr. John D. Mayer, of the University of New Hampshire, and his colleague from Yale University, Dr. Peter Salovey, published two articles on emotional intelligence, formulating the world's first scientific definition of EI. Drawing on their work and that of other researchers, Daniel Goleman, in 1995, wrote a popular book entitled, *Emotional*

Intelligence—Why It Matters More Than IQ. Goleman drew much attention to the topic and deserves a lot of credit for putting the spotlight on this vital aspect of intelligence. All over the world, leaders are rethinking what effective leadership really means, and countless individuals are taking emotional intelligence very seriously as a means of recreating their careers, their relationships and their lives.

Dr. Mayer and Dr. Salovey are internationally regarded scientists in this field, and are the vanguard in measuring emotional intelligence. Their definition of emotional intelligence is a real intelligence; a quite different stance from the popularisations and other academic theories. Psychologists, such as Dr. Robert Sternberg of Yale University, consider it to be the best defined and worked out of the models, a view supported by the fact that the measures grew out of the theory. Their Emotional Intelligence-test, called MSCEIT meets high standards of scientific testing.

This book relies upon the Mayer/Salovey definition, which we'll examine fully in the section, "Emotional Intelligence Defined." There I will explain their four branch model. According to Mayer and Salovey's theory, EI has, above all, to do with recognizing, understanding, dealing with and directing our emotions, and using them as motivators as well. EI is crucial to knowing what we want and what others want, and to optimizing our potential. Having observed thousands of people during twenty years as a leadership consultant and executive coach, it's evident to me that people can more easily create success in their jobs and relationships when they learn to draw on the power of their emotional intelligence and develop emotional skills.

The Art of Leading Yourself will show you how to discover and tap the power of your emotional intelligence. My counsel is based on people's ability to "understand and reason with emotions—as well as to be energized by those feelings," as Dr. John Mayer puts it. By thinking emotionally, we can become better leaders of ourselves and of those around us.

Accessing Your Emotional Intelligence

Getting in touch with your emotional intelligence will make it easier to learn how to manage and lead your life. It's astonishing to see how many of the participants in my seminars are disconnected from their emotional core. Many approach me for help creating a better life for themselves and fulfilling their dreams. They need coaching to get on track to the kind of success and meaning they're searching for. Look at this book as your personal coach.

Emotional intelligence, like cognitive intelligence, is partly inherited and partly a product of education, so the good news is that you can develop your awareness of emotions, just as you can learn in other fields. The tools in this book will help you not only to learn about your EI, but also to harness its powers. Whether you're searching for creativity, professional success, better relationships or peace of mind, this book will guide you to accessing your EI in a way that resonates with your inner voice. In short, it will help you more fully become the person that, somewhere inside, you know you already are.

Leadership

Emotions are contagious. While leadership discussions often focus on the behavior of others, EI requires that we start with leadership of the self. If we see emotions as an individual's core, and agree that an individual can influence others, we naturally conclude that a person's emotions are the key to leadership. Great leaders have the ability not only to relate to and empathize with the emotions of others, but also to recognize and manage their own emotions intentionally and constructively.

"I no longer think that learning how to manage other people, especially subordinates, is the most important thing for executives to learn. I am teaching, above all, how to manage oneself."

— Peter Drucker, American management leader and best-selling author of *The Effective Executive*

A Workbook

You could very well view this as a workbook, and let the concept of work really guide you. As with most kinds of work, there is a payoff, and the payoff here could be the greatest reward of your life. Many people have told me that they've read the entire book, and specific parts of it, a number of times before the ideas took root. The book is also a good basis for stimulating discussions with your colleagues and all the other people you care about.

This book is easy to read, but don't let that fool you. Some of the stories might convey the impression that reaching certain goals is easy, but I can assure you that you'll need to make some very serious choices about the way you live. Creating the life you want takes awareness, time and focus. Be prepared to use the tools offered in this book over a period of time. Try to get involved in what you read; make it matter to you. An occasional urge to throw the book against the wall or out the window might be a signal that you're touching on some important insights about yourself. Often, it's those moments of emotional upheaval and turmoil that force us to confront what's most important to us.

I believe that one day it will be possible for us all to say, as the former president of Iceland, Vigdis Finnbogadottir, did, "When a storm surrounds me, I feel completely calm, because I know who I am and what I want."

Good luck on your journey!

Randi B. Noyes

Questions and Answers

Q: What is Emotional Intelligence?

A: Emotional Intelligence is the intelligent use of thoughts and emotions, heart and mind working harmoniously. It's the ability to use the power of your emotions as a source of information, motivation and connection.

Q: What will Emotional Intelligence do for me?

A: Tapping into your EI will help you solve problems and live a more effective, fulfilling life. It will help you make better choices and deal with people more wisely.

Q: Can it make me smarter or happier?

A: The tools in this book will help you tap more of your intelligence—both IQ and EI. Dealing with your emotions will give you greater happiness and inner peace, and enable you to get rid of that empty spot or the restlessness inside.

Q: Will it get me a better job or a promotion in my present job?

A: What's a better job? Is it one that impresses other people, or one in which you're happier? Using your EI will help you find or create a job that's more *you*, because you'll become more realistic about your strengths, and using your strengths will make you happier.

Q: Will it make me more productive and effective at work?

A: Using your EI to focus on your strengths will help you market the best of yourself instead of pretending to be something you're not. Thus, you'll become more productive and effective in everything you do.

Q: Will it make me a better team player?

A: Yes. Research shows that we need a high level of Emotional Intelligence to be good team players. On any team, you need to understand and deal with your own feelings and reactions and those of your teammates.

Q: Can it improve my relationships; make me a better friend, lover, husband or wife?

A: Tapping your Emotional Intelligence leads to the ability to create trust and be authentic. It's vital to developing good friendships and lasting relationships. If we can't access and manage our emotions, we can't be fully aware of how we influence other people, or interact with others with self-confidence, autonomy and compassionate understanding.

THE ART
of
LEADING YOURSELF

—◆—

Tap the Power of Your
Emotional Intelligence

1

KNOWING YOURSELF

—◆—

LIMITS, POSSIBILITIES AND BREAKING FREE

Once, a baby circus elephant was tied to a heavy stake. The little elephant was so curious, so full of life. He wanted to catch butterflies, look more closely at the flowers that were just out of reach, and play with the children on the grass. Life was an adventure that had to be experienced at that very moment. He jumped up and yanked on his leash again and again, but he couldn't free himself.

This is how we all once were—full of vitality, passion and determination.

Nearby stood the baby elephant's mother. Around her neck was a very thin rope attached to a small stake in the ground. Had she tugged even slightly on the rope, she could have freed herself. But she didn't, having learned long ago that it would have been in vain.

Many of us have also given up, believing that there's no hope of changing our lives.

More than twenty years ago I too had given up hope. Recently divorced, I was living in the United States. I hadn't yet gotten the money for the business I had sold; I was broke and unemployed, and had no promising prospects. My friends, including my best girlfriend, couldn't stand to be with me anymore because of my desperation. It was hard to be around me, but I didn't understand that then.

My family in Norway was disappointed in me and refused to help me in my time of crisis; not even with money for food. By the time they came around, I felt totally alone in the world. My seven-year-old son, who witnessed my plight, declared that he couldn't stand me. I struggled with feelings of fear, desperation, aggression and helplessness—perhaps some of the same feelings you face today. I felt despair as I've never experienced before or since.

I began asking myself some serious questions. Why had I been successful professionally while failing miserably in my private life? Why had my relationships with friends and family deteriorated? What within myself had led me to this low point? I looked everywhere for answers: to career consultants, psychologists, books and friends.

I started exploring my inner self, scrutinizing my soul and personality. Gradually, I was able to see and understand myself more clearly. It was a revealing, exciting journey with fantastic rewards. I managed to calm down and get control of myself, reorganize my life and start a new career that was both successful and meaningful. I had enjoyed financial "success" before, but with an empty feeling inside. Now, my self-confidence was growing, which gave me energy, strength and a fighting spirit in situations where I most needed them.

The lessons I learned on this journey penetrated to the depths of my soul, and are what I want to share with you. They opened my eyes and profoundly changed my life. I have been blessed in many ways, and have gotten more out of life than I ever dreamed possible. The point is to give of oneself generously and without reservation. I didn't know until later that giving is tremendously rewarding and not at all difficult.

In retrospect, it's interesting to see all the pitfalls I once stumbled into. Reading this book can help you detect your own pitfalls and learn how to escape them. When you know where they are, you can avoid them. Sooner or later, everyone falls into a trap. The important question is, will you get out quickly or remain stuck there?

I don't believe in simple solutions. However, if we know the terrain and the map well, it's often possible to find a shortcut. It might be easier than you think. Through my coaching, I see people soar all the time. Now it's your turn.

Of course, I know that every individual is unique, and no two people can travel the same road. My aim is to help you more fully develop *your* individual strengths and build the confidence to make the choices that are optimal for you, even though they may differ from those of others around you or from mine. I want to help you identify those individual strengths of yours that can bring you success, passion and meaning.

When we develop our strengths instead of focusing on our weaknesses, meaningful success is easier than you might think. I've seen the "impossible" happen many times, in my life and in those of other people. Every human being has the potential to experience courage, joy, peace of mind, closeness and love.

> *"If you follow me and do as I do, then you will lose your way, but if you follow your own inclination, you will always find your way."*
> — Ancient adage

Your Inner Voice

We live in a world that incessantly demands greater efficiency, more skill and know-how. The labor market has become increasingly competitive, and there are few guarantees of job

Knowing that I'm responsible for myself and for making my own decisions puts me in the driver's seat; I am the uncontested boss of my life and can never be laid off.

security, especially with more downsizing and reorganization than ever. In this survival-of-the-fittest environment, it's enormously important to have goals and know what you really want to get out of life. Otherwise, you'll feel like a sacrificial lamb on the altar of change.

In my youth, my question was: "What does the world want me to want?" I struggled because the world was constantly changing its mind. Today, it is a relief not to feel dependent on the world's expectations, because I know what I want.

Knowing that I'm responsible for myself and for making my own decisions puts me in the driver's seat; I am the uncontested boss of my life and can never be laid off. This means that I, not other people, determine the course of my life. I make my own choices about my life and about how I want to deal with my circumstances. Believing this, you can begin asking yourself the important questions that help you be more in charge: What do I want? What feels right to me when I'm at peace with myself? What are my values? What's important in the long run?

You'll find a new and easier way to answer these questions as we go along. As a matter of fact, learning how to tap your emotional intelligence will not only answer these questions but will tell you how to make better choices every step of the way.

If you don't know what you want, it's easy for others to take charge of your life; you become like a cork in the middle of the ocean, lost and at the mercy of external forces. If you've taken the time to find out what you want, *you* are leading your life; you are at the steering wheel.

You might be asking yourself: "How can I know for certain what I want?" For many years my primary concern was the expectations of others. It became very simple for me when I learned that we've got to look within ourselves to find the answers. I learned to rely on my inner voice. This book offers you a step-by-step method that has proven valuable for thousands of people. It will take time and extensive practice. Your optimal choices will also benefit those around you sig- *Everyone has this source, an inner voice that can serve as a personal coach.* nificantly. Everyone has this source, an inner voice that can serve as a personal coach. If you ignore this voice for a long time, it becomes weak and nearly impossible to hear. Deep down, we know what's important for us, but we feel completely certain only when we are at peace. Only then can we hear our inner voice clearly. But we are often not at peace; then we stumble along with contradictory forces vying to control us, which is both confusing and tiring.

The most reliable guidance comes from your inner voice, not from books or experts. You can get good ideas from books and other people, but examine them with your inner voice to decide whether you really agree. We are responsible for our lives, whether we choose to accept that responsibility or not. All other responsibilities are optional, but we are responsible for ourselves one hundred percent of the time.

By tapping your emotional intelligence you can be guided from within to take the next step and make the next choice. Just ask yourself how and give yourself the peace you need to hear the answer. The best we can achieve is finding out what's right for ourselves, because no one else can make those judgments for us, though they will try. People might believe that they "know," but they can't *really* know. Why? Because they are not you, so they can never fully understand your inner voice.

To make emotionally intelligent choices, it's important to make sure that it really is your steady, calm inner voice that you're in touch with. If you're relaxed when you "hear it" and it gives you the same message over time, chances are good that it's your inner voice. Avoid mistaking an emotional whim for your inner voice. Such whims can lead you into chaos. Emotional intelligence is the opposite of emotional chaos; it's emotional clarity, when your head and heart are aligned in peaceful knowing, and you are in full agreement with yourself. This is the strong, tranquil message of your inner voice. You can trust your inner voice when you've integrated your negative feelings so that you're calm; you need to have worked through to your positive emotions for your inner voice to be dependable.

If we disregard our inner voice, our road becomes more and more difficult. If you follow your own road, you're safe. If you try to travel someone else's, you'll lose your way time and again.

When pain and anxiety disturb our feelings, we ask ourselves what we really want. When we've made the right choice, our feelings become quiet again. Liv Arnesen, the Norwegian polar explorer, the first woman to conquer the South Pole alone on skis, was asked in an interview what she did when in doubt in the middle of no-man's land. She answered, "I always follow my intuition. I never argue with it. It can be a question of life and death. I have to trust my intuition. It's all I have." When she was in the Antarctic, alone with the forces of nature, Liv had only herself to rely upon. This applies to all of us, even when we're in a crowd of people trying to advise us and make decisions for us. Ultimately, our deep intuition, our inner voice, remains our best guide.

When they read the Norwegian edition of this book, Liv's friends thought that she and I were probably friends, as our ways of thinking were so similar. When Liv heard this, her intuition told her to contact me, which was the start of a great friendship and collaboration. Liv's inner voice has taken her on another expedition in the Antarctic. At this writing, she and Ann Bancroft, from the United States, are on a hundred-day skiing trip across the Antarctic, hauling their own supplies, sleeping in a little tent at night. It might sound crazy to us, but Liv and Ann are following their inner voices and inspiring millions of children all over the world to dare to dream, to dare to follow their inner voice, to live their dreams. Our dreams are vital for a successful life with meaning. Each of us gets unique messages from his or her inner voice. You might do things that other people regard as senseless, but the utmost sign of emotional intelligence is to follow your head and your gut—your own inner voice.

GOD DOESN'T MAKE DEFECTIVE MERCHANDISE

My teacher discovered that I had a reading problem when I had difficulty reading aloud in class. I was twelve years old and ashamed of my disability, so the discovery was really embarrassing for me. I remember thinking that children who could read well were considered bright; I thought I could never be intelligent because of my disability. Hands hot with sweat under my desk, I prayed that I wouldn't have to read aloud, because all the other kids would laugh at me.

I began to think of myself as a piece of defective merchandise and experienced tremendous shame. I compared myself to others constantly in order to gauge my own worth. Who was better, and who worse, prettier, uglier, faster? I've since met many people who have felt this way. Such comparisons can be very destructive to the ego and the inner voice.

After much deliberation I was sent to a speech therapist, then to an actress, Mrs. Sissy Apenes. She was a godsend. We read together, though it was anguish every time. We began reading poetry, and I actually learned to recite quite well. She taught me more than just how to compensate for being unable to read aloud; she found other talents within me and made me aware of them. I believe Mrs. Apenes saved a child, me, that year.

The bitterness and pain of my reading difficulty remained, but grew less important as I developed my true talents and abilities. Often, I thought about how even God could make a mistake, how He could botch things and produce defective merchandise such as me. Later on, perhaps because Mrs. Apenes had planted a seed of faith in me, I was able to change my perspective on my weaknesses. I was not defective, I had merely chosen to see myself in that light. If God had intended me to be a good reader He would have created me differently. My heart's burden lifted when I came to this realization at age nineteen. I decided to concentrate on the things I was capable of rather than on those that I was not. My world became so much more full of meaning and promise; I began seeing opportunities rather than limitations.

You mustn't want it all
You're just one tiny piece
You have your world in the world
This you must make complete

— Piet Hein

YOUR STRENGTH LIES IN WHAT YOU LIKE

You are precisely the way you're supposed to be, and your strength lies inside you. Eventually, these realizations led me to the work I do today, helping people become aware of and concentrate on their talents and skills, which lead them to a richer existence. Using the skills that are driven by your strongest emotions is part of using your emotional intelligence. Tapping that strength brings out tremendous power, and you need this kind of power to create success. We all have strengths and weaknesses: that's reality. Not being good at everything simply confirms that we're human. The challenge is to apply ourselves to what we like and to what comes naturally.

For many years I imported sportswear, a job that required me to visit Europe regularly to acquire new collections of clothing to sell. On the journey, I always conversed with the person seated next to me (in the seventies, more men than women flew across the Atlantic). Unbeknownst to me, the plane was becoming my research laboratory. I couldn't help questioning my neighbor about what he liked to do, what he yearned to do, and what he didn't like doing but did anyway. I soon learned that many people wanted to excel at what they didn't like. My advice to them was (and is) always the same: "Build on your strengths, not on your weaknesses. Concentrate on what you are passionate about or you'll just be mediocre."

"Build on your strengths, not on your weaknesses. Concentrate on what you are passionate about or you'll just be mediocre."

Before landing in Copenhagen or Boston, our conversation had inevitably revealed a lot about my fellow passenger's true abilities and interests. This was a unique and very exciting opportunity to understand human nature.

Then, remarkably, I began to get letters and calls from all over the world. People thanked me for the conversations we'd had, and told me how transformative they had been. From call after call I learned that people were taking charge of their lives by doing the things that reflected their strengths and passions. The businessman who called from New York had started his own bookstore; my cleaning woman began studying philosophy; our babysitter started manufacturing handbags. When I heard from the woman in Ghana who had become head of a thirty-person company, and when calls poured in from Paris and Milan, I finally understood that I had an idea that could be *my* calling, something that would be meaningful and enjoyable for me and for others. The passion for my dream grew.

After realizing that I could offer the world something that truly interested me, the work of making it a reality became my challenge. The epiphany was wonderful, as it connected my skills and passions and gave me a meaningful goal. Still, implementing that goal demanded commitment and focus. There were many questions to answer and much to learn. I worked with psychologists, a career counselor, leadership consultant LeRoy Malouf (my mentor), business leaders and theorists, all of whom challenged me in new and different ways, broadening my perspective. While all that I was learning changed my ideas every day, my objective remained constant: I wanted to give seminars on resource

10

The challenge was to take the time and effort to develop what was strong, instead of improving on what wasn't.

finding and self-management. I was still far from understanding how to truly tap emotional intelligence; I had grasped just a tiny part of it.

The first "People in Focus" seminar was held at a friend's house in 1980. That was the test. People were excited and felt they had learned something important. I knew then that I had a good idea, though it needed significant development. Then I advertised, and my first official seminar took place. Because of press coverage, I received over eighty calls, but only one caller could afford to pay. The seminar was held anyway.

I knew that this was what I really wanted. Leading seminars about resource development and mapping out strengths and weaknesses came naturally to me, perhaps because of my own struggles. I believed that my career, and the responses of my former colleagues and flight partners, confirmed one important thing: everyone had something special. The challenge was to take the time and effort to develop what was strong, instead of improving on what wasn't. That, I believed, would bring faster, better results and much enjoyment, while the latter resulted in mediocrity at best.

One of my most dependable advisors was Ursula Willis, a woman of abundant warmth and common sense. A career consultant, she helped people discover their resources and market themselves effectively. One day, Ursula had her clients write what they *liked* to do on little scraps of yellow paper. Then she had them write what they *didn't* like to do on blue scraps. When everyone had finished, she sat on the windowsill, enthusiastically reading aloud from the yellow scraps, reading each and placing it carefully on a neat pile. She read the blue scraps ponderously, and one by one threw them out the window. That image still remains with me. Occasionally, I pester myself with blue scraps, but when I recognize one, I immediately head for the window to throw it away. I encourage you to identify and treasure your yellow scraps and let your blue ones go.

The Art of Leading Yourself

Some people know what they want to be from a very young age. Most of us, however, become educated and find jobs without ever figuring it out, mainly because we're unaware of our gifts and abilities. Many of us end up feeling inadequate at our jobs, because we pursue careers that are so out of sync with what we're meant to be doing. Often, we perceive our difficulty as an indication that we're not intelligent enough. It's impossible to be talented at everything, and if we hope or expect to, we ensure disappointment and frustration. Instead, we're much better off pursuing what we're good at and what we enjoy.

Many business leaders come to me to tap their greatest strengths and deepest passions. Often, they don't know that this is exactly what we're going to do. They come because they want more meaning in their lives, and they wouldn't mind more financial success as well.

Many business leaders come to me to tap their greatest strengths and deepest passions. Often, they don't know that this is exactly what we're going to do. They come because they want more meaning in their lives, and they wouldn't mind more financial success as well.

How many times have you wished you could have someone else's talents, or felt jealous of people who show off their talents? When we feel confident in our own abilities, we feel far less threatened by the abilities of others. In fact, their talents can inspire us. We are meant to be different, and we need to learn to embrace our own unique qualities. Difference creates opportunities.

Many people want others to discover for them what they are best suited to do in their professional lives. You, however, have the potential to understand yourself better than anyone else can. Few people can give you good advice, and it's very risky to put your fate in someone else's hands. Ultimately, you're the one with the insight and the motivation to understand yourself. You need to embrace this responsibility, and I would like to help you in the effort.

It can sometimes appear that two people have identical

talents, but I challenge this assertion. Analyzing people's talents and abilities is like comparing fingerprints; no two are alike. I have mapped the strengths of thousands of people. I treasure their uniqueness, and am convinced that we are supposed to be exactly as we are. The sooner we find careers that correspond to our true selves, the better and richer our lives will be. We will be more successful and better rewarded if we match our careers to our interests and talents.

Are you asking yourself, "How can I know what I'm good at?" I believe that you already know, though you might not be able to articulate it yet. Dwelling on what they aren't good at sidetracks many people, so they don't spend the necessary time trying to discover and develop their aptitudes. We all have our "precious stones." When we are unfamiliar with our gems, we can't display them effectively. I want to help you learn how to successfully mine your precious stones.

Start by asking yourself some simple questions: What do I enjoy doing? What gives me the most pleasure? What kinds of activities come easily and naturally to me? What am I passionate about? When you can answer these questions truthfully, you'll have uncovered your gemstones. Remember, what you enjoy doing is your resource, and what you *love* to do is your greatest resource of all. Our resources emanate from us, whether we want them to or not. If you pay close attention to the choices you make and the things you naturally gravitate toward, you'll see that you're revealing your resources.

Part of the difficulty in understanding our resources is that we can't really see ourselves. We take our talents for granted; using them feels so easy that we forget to give ourselves credit for having them. When I ask you to consider the activities that make you happy, it's because I know you'll find a talent there. Yet, we rarely think that what makes us happy is profound enough to give us the understanding we're looking for. You can gain some insight from the lists in Chapter 6. Keep in mind that they aren't simply lists of wants and wishes. If you select what you like to do, I guarantee that you've got some ability there.

Once you've written the words that you feel describe you, go over the lists again. Then, draw a circle around the words that strike a strong chord inside you because they fit so well with how you experience life. Those words describe you; you're passionate about them. They describe what will catapult you to where you want to be. They give you power. Have a conversation with yourself about the words you recognize in yourself; explore them more fully. How do they relate to the way you live your life?

It's also helpful to examine what you've eliminated from this list. Many of these words will steal your energy instead of empowering you. What you don't like to do can help you identify your talents and passions and also help you to steer clear of focusing your efforts on activities that don't make you happy, and produce results that are average at best. Far too many people spend years doing what they dislike. Whether urged by their parents, who hope to realize their own unfulfilled dreams through their children, or looking for prestige and respect, they will find it difficult or impossible to be successful, and their efforts will lack joy and meaning.

By working with these lists, you might find two or three groups of resources. You'll be well on the way to finding yourself, and your precious stones will begin to become visible to you. Then you can start to plan realistically, and only then can you market yourself effectively. Please identify what you like to do and how you'd do it if you were fully free to decide. They are your "gems."

After you've completed these lists, try talking with someone you trust. Discussing these personal discoveries can bring new understanding. But remember to sift all the good advice you receive through your inner voice. Does your rational mind like the idea? More importantly, does it feel right? Ultimately, you are the source of wisdom about yourself. This understanding brings us a little closer to what emotional intelligence is.

Some readers might feel disappointed early in the process, because they think they should discover a great new talent immediately. I promise that you *will* find a talent, but only when you can see and accept yourself as you really are. Trying to become something we are not casts a shadow over our true potential. Denial and deceit make our talents invisible.

Not long ago my friend Joe called me and asked for advice. "Randi, what shall I do? I'm really split. I think I ought to start a business now, because I've got so much experience at what I do and soon I'll be too old to do it."

"The real issue isn't whether you're getting too old or how much experience you have. Do you really want to start a business?" I asked.

"I think it might be smart, because I'm tired of letting all the money I earn for my company go into their pockets."

"Joe, I've never mapped your strengths, but I have some questions to start you off: How long have you wanted to start a business? Have you thought about it often or is the idea new to you?"

"Well, I just thought it could be a good idea!"

"OK, you think it's a smart idea, but how does starting your own business *feel?*" It was quiet at the other end for some time. I figured he was checking his feelings. "It doesn't feel that good!"

"Do you really think you can succeed at something you don't feel good about?"

Joe and I had a long discussion about his strengths and how he could live his dreams wherever he chose. He has managed to do just that.

It's awful to do things we don't love doing! Sometimes, a dream grows stronger over time; then, when it feels right, it's because it probably *is* the right thing to pursue. You can be inspired to find out what you really want to do by the advice once given by the great German author Rainer Maria Rilke in his *Letters to a Young Poet:*

You ask whether your verses are any good. You ask me. You have asked others before this. You send them to magazines. You compare them with other poems, and you are upset when certain editors reject your work. Now (since you have said you want my advice) I beg you to stop doing that sort of thing. You are looking outside, and that is what you should most avoid right now. No one can advise or help you - no one. There is only one thing you should do. Go into yourself. Find out the reason that commands you to write; see whether it has spread its roots into the very depths of your heart; confess to yourself whether you would have to die if you were forbidden to write. This most of all: ask yourself in the most silent hour of your night: must I write? Dig into yourself for a deep answer. And if this answer rings out in assent, if you meet this solemn question with a strong, simple "I must," then build your life in accordance with this necessity; your whole life, even into its humblest and most indifferent hour, must become a sign and witness to this impulse . . .

Finally, I want to add just one more bit of advice: to keep growing, silently and earnestly, through your whole development; you couldn't disturb it any more violently than by looking outside and waiting for outside answers to questions that only your innermost feeling, in your quietest hour, can perhaps answer.

— (Translation by Stephen Mitchell)

Unfortunately, many of us learned in childhood to suppress our natural inclinations. With the best of intentions, our parents encouraged us to follow the safe, pedestrian, route rather than encouraging us to gamble on the talents we really wanted to develop.

An extremely creative engineer who came to one of my seminars was able to see situations and ask questions from angles no one else in the room had considered. Unfortunately, he asked

all his questions in a disturbingly aggressive manner. I genuinely appreciated the questions, which stimulated us all to think
in new and different ways, but I couldn't understand why his
approach was so aggressive. When he understood my sincere
appreciation of his challenging questions, he began to open
up. He said that his mother had constantly scolded him for
asking too many questions as a child; this had made him re-
strain himself. I could so clearly picture this curious child—a
boy with an uncanny ability to ask questions—being stifled.
Now, as an adult, when he did ask questions, he felt a need to
be forceful, anticipating a similar scolding. Through our conversation, he relived many feelings about his childhood and
his inability to embrace his curiosity. I was deeply moved when
he began to understand that asking questions was one of his
most valuable resources, to be treasured rather than suppressed.
As we worked through the antiquated attitudes he had been
subjected to, and stressed the new, positive view of curiosity,
he began to feel more comfortable, asking questions calmly
and respectfully. Today, he works in product development, precisely
because he can play the role of devil's advocate so effectively,
seeing every situation from many different angles, spurring
creativity in himself and others.

When, in another seminar, we were asked to put a check
next to the words that best described what we liked doing,
something unexpected happened. I had told the participants
never to doubt that what they liked to do was a resource. Jeanne,
a thirty-year-old woman, raised her hand for help in checking
off the words that best described her resources. She'd been
silent most of the day, and when she whispered her question
in my ear, I realized that she had a stutter. "I l-l-like to p-p-per-
form. Is this a resource I have?" Concerned about how best to
respond, I nearly told her that I wasn't sure, but stopped myself. "Of course acting is your resource—you like it, don't you?"
She seemed relieved. As we neared the end of the session, I
handed out exercises for the following day. I asked Jeanne if

she would like to give a twenty-minute talk about something that was important to her. She said yes, but stuttered terribly when we discussed it.

The next morning, Jeanne arrived, wearing new clothes and having cut her hair. This was obviously an important moment for her. She stood up in front of us, twelve people in all, holding a manuscript in her hand, and slowly began, "I was four years old when I first began to stutter." All of us were anxiously wondering how this would play out. A few moments later, we seemed to forget ourselves, entranced by a truly gripping story. "My parents tried to discipline away my stuttering, but with each scolding it just got worse. They asked other family members to discourage my stuttering, but all the attention to my handicap only made it worse."

Jeanne talked about the knot that would form in her stomach when she heard herself stutter, about her shame when people teased her. As an adult, her stuttering interfered so dramatically with her life that when she saw someone she knew on the street, she'd pretend not to recognize them, and run away to avoid speaking. Stuttering became such a burden that she had no choice but to take action. She went to a speech therapist, which proved to be of some help. Now she was willing to do *anything* to get rid of her speech impediment forever. She had come to the conclusion that she had to do what she feared most: speak in front of an audience. Ironically, she had always dreamed of being some kind of performer.

With a mixture of joy and dread, Jeanne stood before our group. She stuttered at the beginning, but gradually both she and the audience forgot about it. The experience was a powerful one for all of us. Jeanne had finally mustered the courage to stand face to face with her handicap in order to put it behind her. We were all amazed to watch her stutter fade, and it continued fading long after she left the seminar. I later received a long, happy letter from her, saying that she had been asked to make formal presentations for her company. To do

To do what we really want, sometimes we have to overcome great obstacles. what we really want, sometimes we have to overcome great obstacles.

When I was preparing to give a seminar for some executives fifteen years ago, I spent six months getting ready, and it still made me very nervous. Each time I bathed, I'd picture all those powerful people. In my mind they were all tough and ill tempered. With each bath, I tried to change the image, visualizing them as more relaxed and pleasant. By the time the seminar took place, the reality was a pleasant surprise. The seminar was a success, and the participants proved quite interesting and challenging. Those intense fears have never returned.

YOU AND YOUR JOB

Finding your unique strengths in both your personal and professional life is ultimately your own responsibility. Sadly, most businesses and organizations don't help employees to identify their personal resources. We can't afford to wait for others to uncover our talents. Instead, we have to find our hidden gems ourselves and learn to take full advantage of them. Ironically, many people don't properly appreciate their talents, because those gifts come very easily to them. It's hard for people to imagine success emerging from talents and abilities that come naturally and with little effort. It's important to bear in mind that what comes easily to one may be an impossibility to another.

We need to remember and accept that we can't be good at everything and that other people can do some things better than we can. That's life, and while we have to accept it, we're not obliged to emphasize it publicly. Because of our insecurities, we often broadcast our ignorance rather than choosing to emphasize our knowledge and talents.

With so much uncertainty in the job market, we need to be ready for change and prepared to meet its challenges dynamically and constructively. The first lesson is to know ourselves: our interests, abilities, talents, dreams, habits and style. Only then do we have a stable foundation for dealing with the challenges confronting us. No one can successfully confront a world in constant change without knowing their own strengths and what they really want. Remember that you are exactly the way you're supposed to be, and you have enough resources to create your special type of success and a meaningful life.

No one can successfully confront a world in constant change without knowing their own strengths and what they really want.

TAKING RESPONSIBILITY FOR YOUR OWN LIFE

During my first marriage, plentiful evidence seemed to justify my blaming my husband for all our marital problems. From his perspective, of course, *I* was the one to blame for everything that was wrong. We lived in a vicious circle of mutual accusation. I spent a great deal of energy pointing out all his shortcomings until, one day while driving, I heard a voice on the radio say that people are responsible for their own lives. The truth of it struck me immediately. I knew intuitively that the speaker was right. That insight affected me profoundly, and proved to be a turning point in my life.

But what did it really mean to take responsibility for one's own life? I thought about my unhappiness and whom I had considered responsible for it: my husband and my parents. Were they in fact *not* accountable for my unhappiness and the miserable state of my marriage? I realized that this was exactly what the voice on the radio had meant—I, and I alone, was responsible for my life and my feelings. There was no one else to blame. I stood alone; I was responsible for my own life.

At first I felt lonely and afraid, completely alone in the United States, without money or job, and with everyone around me seemingly expecting something of me. I was also responsible for my young son. As this realization sank in, my fear began to turn into strength. This was *my* responsibility and *my* life. *I* could make the choices that were right for me. If we aren't responsible for our lives, I wouldn't have the freedom to choose, but we are and do. I began to feel freer and more in control of my life, embracing the responsibility instead of shying away from it. I decided that if my father continued intruding in my life and making demands on me, I would ask him to pay my bills. Unless someone else wanted the responsibility of paying for my life, they were certainly not entitled to interfere and try to control it. From now on I would live according to my own precepts and inclinations, according to directions from my heart, not from external demands. I alone would pay my bills, and I would live with the consequences of the choices I made.

What will it mean for you to take responsibility for *your* life? That's what you'll find out in this book. I hope your quest will be as liberating for you as mine has been. When you fully appreciate the fact that you alone are responsible for your life, you'll feel as if a heavy iron ball and chain has dropped from your ankle. You'll feel a sudden new freedom, a dynamic, exciting challenge. The next moment, you might feel, as I did, that it's a heavy burden to bear.

There are many things in life that we can't control: We can't change the past; the childhood we had; our parents who, with the best of intentions, sometimes treated us unwisely; the current market situation; the jobs we've lost; and so on. Should you feel responsibility for all this? The answer is no. We can't be responsible for injustices—real or imagined—suffered in the past, but we are responsible now for how we choose to think about or deal with them. If we can't control events, we'd better focus our attention and apply our energies to the things we can influence.

Because you can't control the world, you needn't carry its weight on your shoulders. You do, however, have control over yourself, and responsibility for yourself and your life whether you choose to take it or not, and you have to live with the consequences of your own choices.

Taking responsibility for your life implies being free, every second of the day, to choose how you'll deal with yourself, with other people, with any situations in the world. You have that freedom whether you believe it or not. If you can take this freedom and use it wisely, making good, solid choices, you'll have the greatest impact on your life and on the world around you. The power to choose is yours.

Taking responsibility for your life implies being free, every second of the day, to choose how you'll deal with yourself, with other people, with any situations in the world.

A few years ago I received a letter from Britha, who was twenty-eight years old and had experienced a lot of trouble in her life:

It wasn't until I read your book that I understood how important it was to take responsibility for my own life. I was unaware that I am totally responsible for my own life, though I knew it on some level. Now that I have awakened, I know it is important to know what *I* want. I am willing to lead myself and be in charge of my life. Before, I used sit in the back seat instead of at the steering wheel. For a while, I knew that I was steering, but I had a setback. I fell in love and, strangely, chose to take the back seat again. It was terrible. I didn't understand at first what I had chosen—it was as if I was sleepwalking. When I woke up, I took my place at the steering wheel of my life again. I feel much better after having been able to share with my boyfriend that I want to be in charge of my life; that he is free to choose what's right for him, but only I can decide what's right or wrong for me to do in my life. Thank you for waking me from my sleep. I feel more optimistic now that I know I'm free to decide what I want to do. I hope I won't choose to retreat to the back seat again because I want to make a great life for myself and for the people I love. I can only be a giving person if I take responsibility

for my life and my feelings! That will enable me to have a
lot to give to others.

RESPONSIBILITY

There are many types of responsibility. We've talked about
the most basic and most important one, responsibility for
your own life. By taking the freedom this allows, you'll have
more to give: you'll be more honest, you'll take better care of
yourself, you won't blame others, you'll set limits, you'll be
more authentic, and you'll be aware of the importance of your
choices and their effects on you and other people. Our problems arise when we pretend not to be responsible for our
own life, that someone else—our parents, our spouse, our
boss or society—is.

When you take responsibility for your life, you ask yourself,
what do I *choose* to do for family, for children, for society?
Responsibility becomes different when you *choose* it. Being
responsible for your own life will help you decide what kinds
of responsibilities you want to say yes to, and choose where,
when and how you'll commit to being active.

YOUR EXPECTATIONS—AND THEIRS

Expectations are complicated. We expect things of ourselves
and from others and they of us. In addition we face moral or
religious expectations. These latter are highly personal and concern complicated issues that fall outside the scope of this book.

Sometimes it's hard to decide whether the expectations we
feel are reasonable. We might imagine that people expect something
from us when in fact they don't. Hoping to be liked or ad-
mired, we sometimes try to satisfy unspoken expectations that
exist only in our imagination. When you take complete responsibility for your life, you can choose whether to strive to
live up to those expectations—expressed or unexpressed. This

can be a difficult choice, but it's a necessary one.

It's easy to imagine how the world "ought to" be for me to be happy; how my boyfriend or husband ought to be so that our relationship could improve; or what my boss ought to have done that he didn't do. It's alarming to acknowledge how many "ought to" expressions arise in our vocabulary, and it's revelatory to realize that "ought to" territory exists only in our minds. Considerations of what ought to have happened are irrelevant. Your boss didn't behave as you thought she should; she simply was as she was.

The concept of "ought to" distracts you from what's real. The sooner you accept what actually took place, the easier it will be to deal with the reality confronting you. By taking responsibility for living in the real world rather than a world of hopes and illusions, you become better able to take charge of your life. It takes time and effort to fully come to terms with this idea. When you do, you'll realize how much more powerful an impact you have on your life.

Peter had been angry with his father for quite some time. He felt that his father ought to have planned how to subsidize Peter's education long before the time came for him to go to school. I asked Peter whether he enjoyed being so angry, especially considering that his father couldn't undo what had already happened. Peter was having a hard time accepting the reality of his situation: his father had just gone bankrupt and simply had no money.

His father's failure turned out to be a blessing in disguise. When Peter finally began to accept the reality of his father's poor planning, unexpected possibilities arose for him. The shortage of money meant that Peter had to get a job. He chose one related to his field of study, which led to an exciting career opportunity after he finished college. Once he had made the conscious decision to assume the responsibility for his own choices, what his father "ought to" have done no longer mattered. The key for Peter was determining what he himself could

Let's accept the fact that we miss the mark sometimes and that we have the right to do so. If one of our goals is to become warmer and more loving, then learning to be patient with ourselves means that we'll be kinder and more forgiving toward other people.

do to improve his situation.

Usually, *we* make the greatest demands on ourselves. Many people continually reproach themselves because they "ought to" be more effective, "ought to" visit their aging mother more often, "ought to" go on a diet, "ought to" be kinder and better and *get themselves together!* Paradoxically, the more we harp on all we "ought to" have done, the more the problem affects us. When life becomes an "I ought to" affair, we continually feel inadequate. We lose contact with ourselves and with our potential, and undermine our self-confidence.

Let's accept the fact that we miss the mark sometimes and that we have the right to do so. If one of our goals is to become warmer and more loving, then learning to be patient with ourselves means that we'll be kinder and more forgiving toward other people. This is really the foundation of a life filled with love. If you can embrace the ideas "I am as I am, right at this moment" and "I could not have done better at that moment," you begin creating a kinder, more beautiful world. Life gets easier when you no longer expect that you or others "ought to" be different. When we can disengage ourselves from "ought to," we can base our choices on what's real right now. At that point we become empowered to influence today and the future in a powerful, meaningful way.

THE CHILD IS PERFECT

A normal, healthy child is a wonder of nature and a blessing to parents. Although some children are born with handicaps, most arrive fully equipped, all their faculties intact. In the eyes of their parents, they're perfect. It isn't until later, when we begin to compare our children's achievements with those of other people's children, that this view may be challenged.

This became real to me when my son came home with his first report card: one good grade, the rest awful! I was deeply disappointed. I, who had vigorously asserted that every child is perfect, now had to come to terms with the hard facts of life. I knew it was important to stress the positive. After a while, I calmed down. "Look how good you are in math! I'm so proud of you," I said. And I meant it. I was genuinely proud of my little son who was so good at math. For both of us, I continued emphasizing all that was good about my son—that he was a wonderful friend, that he was tactful, that he drew well—the list just grew longer and longer, and finding each other's good points became a game of ours.

It pleased me to see how this little game bolstered his self-esteem. He became more courageous and open to trying new activities. Concentrating on what he was good at gave him the confidence to pursue those things and to develop other aspects of himself. He has now completed college and graduate school and has an insatiable desire to live and learn.

As a child, my nephew Jacob was different from all the other kids in the family. He showed no inclination to sit or crawl at the appropriate age; he was content to just lie in his crib. Everyone wondered what would happen to Jacob. "He is exactly as he should be," his mother said. "There's nothing wrong with him." With time, and in his own special way, Jacob proved to be the family's philosopher. When he was five years old, he told me excitedly, "Know what, Aunt Randi? When I meet people, they tell me everything they're good at, and I tell them everything I'm good at, and then we're twice as clever. Isn't that smart?" His calm, thoughtful manner made him approachable. Though he wasn't quite like other children, Jacob's parents thought he was perfect the way he was. This kind of belief, acceptance and support provided the atmosphere for genuine development. Today, Jacob is a bright young man with a profound perspective on the world.

Often, parents don't fully appreciate their children as they are. Ellen Goodman is an exceptional journalist who, in one of her articles for *The Boston Globe,* stressed the importance of stimulating young children and teenagers, and warns parents against the "worry-comparison syndrome." If children show ability in athletics, parents compare them to those who excel in theoretical subjects. If children study too much, parents worry about them not making the basketball or football team. If they show an aptitude for music, their parents become concerned whether they're good enough at math. The serious, contemplative ones are sure to be compared to those who are more lighthearted and carefree; but if they enjoy life too much, then the parents will worry about them not being serious enough.

I recall meeting a little girl in Florida some years ago. A year and a half old, she was still in her baby carriage. She stared intensely at me, so intensely that I had a visceral reaction: I wanted to move away from her. Experience has taught me that I'm in touch with a resource when something emanates so strongly from a person, but in this case I had no idea what the resource was. I didn't understand what I was experiencing. Instead of avoiding the child, I spoke to her mother. "What an interesting child you have," I said, "She has something special that I don't have the words to describe." "She's interesting all right," the mother responded, "The only thing is, she can't speak."

That response tells us a lot about the perspective of parents. We have a tendency to pay attention to what a child is missing, instead of focusing on his or her abilities. Although an unusual ability can be unsettling, it's important for parents to find out how to help their children harness their abilities and use them constructively.

The little girl's mother was a researcher who spent hours every day looking into a microscope. It struck me that this child could see, really see, and grasp the details and nuances of life. She had probably inherited this ability from her mother, who used it every day in her work. Few individuals can really see the world. Try to draw just a tiny part of a tree trunk and you'll know what I mean. Where some of us may need to capture a scene on film to remember it, others retain it naturally and effortlessly.

If we don't appreciate ourselves as we are, we reduce our potential for happiness. By choosing to dwell on what we're not capable of rather than what we're good at, we become unable to feel gratitude or joy about our talents. I sincerely hope that you'll discover, appreciate and accept the best in yourself and in others.

RELATIONSHIP TO MOTHER AND FATHER

Many psychologists believe that difficult and painful feelings can be traced back to infancy. Some have expressed it like this: First we were hurt, and because we couldn't put our pain into words, it became anger, and because we had no outlet for our anger, our anger became anguish.

PAIN—ANGER—ANGUISH

We all bear scratches and scars from childhood. This isn't that our parents or others *wanted* to hurt us, but because human beings aren't always capable of unconditional love. Unable to understand this, children feel only the pain associated with loss of love. Some psychologists believe that this pain is our own choice, and that lack of love is its foundation.

There are plenty of theories on the subject. Interestingly, many of the experts fail to agree. I choose to believe that you and I were full of love when we were born—the most constructive approach to the question, given that no one really knows the truth.

The Bible says that we are made in the image of God. It's also written that God is love. As I see it, the newborn baby is the fruit and expression of love, and then faces the challenge of living with mother and father.

When I began studying psychology, I wasn't aware of how much our parents influence our lives. Many people who attend my seminars gain valuable and unexpected insights as we begin to analyze how our parents and other people actually dominate our thinking as young people—and still do even in our adulthood. I'll try to highlight the essential elements of the enormous literature on the subject.

It's impossible for us to find peace of mind or complete happiness as long as we cling to resenting our parents. Resentment continues to control our lives if we don't actively free ourselves of it. We can't become free of our parents by blaming or resenting them. The idea that we tend to dislike those whom we most resemble holds especially true with parental figures. If we continue to judge them, we deny ourselves the knowledge of our similarities to them, especially in the ways we criticize most strongly.

Years ago, it was widely believed that thirty percent of the population had unresolved issues with their parents. From experience, I believe it's closer to ninety percent. When someone in anguish comes to one of my seminars, my first question is whether they're angry with one of their parents. I'm rarely mistaken in this approach. Their responses reveal a lot of self-deception: "Years ago I accepted the fact that my parents are the way they are, and there's no sense trying to change them. I'm comfortable with the situation now." Such rationalization and denial characterizes many parent-child relationships. Ultimately, such prolonged binding to the parents can severely impede an individual's personal growth.

Another coping mechanism may be effusive praise for parents. Elise, a thirty-four-year-old, told me that she still lived at home, because her mother and father were "so fantastic." I didn't probe this issue deeply the first day—everyone is entitled to what they believe—and her parents might have been great people. What was obvious, however, was that she wasn't yet free from her parents. I respected Elise's attitude, and gave her plenty of room in the seminar to think clearly and make decisions that felt right to her. On the second day of the seminar she exclaimed, "I hate them!" "Who?" I asked, somewhat confused, because we hadn't been talking about anyone in particular. "Mom and Dad. I hate them!"

Does this story strike a chord in you? We are taught that our lives will be good and happy if we honor our mother and father. I believe, however, that to be true to this precept, we must first acknowledge our true feelings and cleanse ourselves of any remaining anger and resentment. That's the emotionally intelligent thing to do. On my advice, Elise wrote a number of angry letters to her parents, but didn't mail them. By expressing her feelings through writing, she was able to confront her deeply buried emotions and get rid of much of her pain. She became better able to live according to her own deep wishes and view of life instead of those of her parents. This process can take a lot of time, but it's essential to becoming a more emotionally integrated and whole human being.

If you have problematic relationships with your parents, I urge you to do the same exercise. Write a hundred letters if you need to, until you've seen through your aggression and reached the core of your heartfelt love, but don't mail any of them. After you express your painful feelings honestly, forgiveness comes. When you get close to this core, you'll be truly able to honor and love your parents, not because you feel obligated to, but because it will come naturally to you.

On the surface, Jerry seemed the complete opposite of Elise, but it turned out that they were actually very much alike. The critical difference was that Elise had suppressed much of her aggression, while Jerry was furious at everything and everyone (including me). I listened and listened and, finally, he began to trust me.

Bit by bit, Jerry revealed his tender side. He admitted that he'd been taking out his anger and aggression on his four-year-old daughter. He became furious and outraged when she didn't want to brush her teeth. Obviously, it's unfair to unleash aggression on an innocent, helpless four-year-old.

Jerry was a deeply hurt man, and therefore a very angry man, and the cause of his fury was buried deep inside him. It was no surprise to find out that his relationship with his parents was terribly unhealthy. Whenever they were in his house, Jerry turned into an ogre. The challenge was to find the source of his anger and an acceptable outlet for it.

Jerry wrote and wrote, which proved to be a great help. He had found a less destructive way to channel his anger. I recommended mental training to help him defuse the anger rather than act it out. Also, I advised him to see a psychologist, because he needed the ongoing support and guidance of a professional. Willingness to seek professional help is a sign that people are prepared to take responsibility for their lives. Later, when Jerry came to a follow-up seminar, he told us that his situation was much better and that he no longer feared his emotions. His dedicated work with himself had enabled him to integrate his emotions and made him wiser and more peaceful. He was now able to harness the emotional intelligence we need to make a better life for ourselves.

Such a process takes time, and we need to allow ourselves to take that time. We deserve to congratulate ourselves each time we bravely confront our feelings instead of running away from them and trying not to feel.

Many people dread the task of giving up the resentment they feel toward their parents, despite their understanding that they won't reach their potential in life unless they let go of these feelings. Whenever you feel blocked, angry or hurt, work through those feelings, acknowledge them and analyze them fully. Try to sense where they are in your body. What do you feel? What other feelings are hiding behind the initial feelings? What do they tell you? Be patient with yourself—you're working with an important tool that will help you tap your emotional intelligence.

As adults, when we've been hurt or slighted, we can put our feelings into words. As children, when a wound was originally inflicted on us, we were unable to do so. Moreover, we continue to be hurt time and again when someone pours salt on that original wound. Some people even assert that we can't feel hurt as adults unless we were hurt in a similar way in childhood. Whatever the origin of our wounds, by fully feeling and experiencing them we are more capable of healing them. In time, our emotional injuries can be fully healed. The uncontrollable anger that sometimes comes from touching an old wound tells us that we're getting close to the source of the trouble. Our feelings are always intelligent; they tell us what's going on, and it's wise to take them seriously. What we *do* in the heat of emotion is often not so intelligent, but it's smart to pay attention to the messages our feelings give us. Anger provides wonderful clues to resolving emotional conflicts. It can be a way to find the core of our wounds, to feel them fully, to understand them and, ultimately, be able to cleanse and heal them.

When we reveal our sore spots and share them with others, personal relationships develop and improve; we can see one another more clearly.

When we reveal our sore spots and share them with others, personal relationships develop and improve; we can see one another more clearly. It's vital that we experience our wounds completely, without protection, so that we can describe them to ourselves and to others. This will help us heal our souls. If we neglect to make contact with all the feelings associated with a wound, and don't relive the original incident, then the injury might never disappear. To feel wounded is to have a hidden, sensitive spot that can become energized. We have emotional memory. If our boss speaks to us in a way that's similar to the way our father did, and we experienced that as painful in childhood, we will feel the pain again. When we confront our vulnerability, we become stronger. By moving through the pain and not circumventing it, we become whole human beings.

In addition to genetic factors, we are, to a great extent, what we are and where we are as a result of the choices, both conscious and unconscious, that we've made up to the present moment.

An early stage in coaching leaders is to map what kinds of wounds stand in their way. I always find some, and the leaders I work with become better leaders when they have neutralized their hot buttons. The next step is to give attention daily to what you feel, in order to manage the emotions as they happen. Being aware of your emotions is the key, then feeling them, then having them tell you what they have to say. You learn to listen to yourself, and take signals from yourself and others seriously. That is a self-leadership tool we all need to develop; that's using your emotional intelligence.

It's comforting to share our thoughts and feelings with those we love and respect. Doing so heals wounds and relieves pain. If you're in trouble, don't hesitate to ask someone you care about to listen to your inner feelings. Tell them that you need them to be there and simply listen to you. Tell them that you don't expect any advice. Often, it's more than sufficient that your friend simply listen.

Negative Feelings Breed Negative Results

During twenty years of conducting seminars, I've asked thousands of people how they cope with adversity. "What do you do to pick yourself up when you've had a hard day? How do you cope with difficulty?"

The answers varied. Different methods seemed to work, and what worked for one person didn't necessarily work for another. What remained constant, however, was agreement that only *you* can pick yourself up. If someone doesn't want to be helped, most efforts are futile. In addition to genetic factors, we are, to a great extent, what we are and where we are as a result of the choices, both conscious and unconscious, that we've made up to the present moment. Our own will and choice determine what happens to us. Some people feel that they're totally at mercy of other people's choices. While this might feel true for many of us, we are responsible for our own lives and we are not at the mercy of others. We can ask for help, but we have to do the job ourselves. We can influence, and we can make new choices that will in turn lead to different results.

Most leaders who want my coaching are interested in improving their leadership skills. They're already very good at what they do. Occasionally, a really sad leader looks me up. I choose whom I want to coach with care. I'm looking for leaders who are willing to "pay the price," to do whatever is necessary to create the life they want. I can teach them tools and ask the right questions to coach them to greater success and meaning, but I can't lift anyone. The leader has to do the homework that we've mutually agreed upon to ensure progress. I teach my clients to lift themselves.

Michael, a business leader I worked with, began using the visual image of being either under or on top of the table. We needed to use tools for getting "onto the tabletop and higher." One such helpful technique is to scream, to "stand in the feelings" for a while and exaggerate them, so that they slowly become milder and we can visualize ourselves climbing up on top of the table. Checking where you are right now—under, on the edge of the table, on top or even higher—is a good test of how you're doing. It's healthy to do some check-ins on your feelings as the day goes by. Then you can meet them, integrate them and move on. This is a way to assure that you're tapping into and using your emotional intelligence to influence yourself and your world the way you want to.

Our feelings change constantly. In the course of any day, we might feel happy, calm, bitter, aggressive, or irritated. Negative feelings weigh heavily on us, and if we don't manage them they can keep us down in times of trouble.

How can we lift ourselves up when we choose to? When life gets rough, there are nearly as many methods to apply as there are people in the world. Some go jogging when pressure builds up; life feels easier after a good sweat. Some find taking a walk helpful, while others listen to music or do woodworking. Still others chop down trees, releasing frustration with every blow— plenty of good therapy there. Some people prefer having long conversations with themselves.

Before my divorce, I exhausted my friends by talking incessantly when I was hurt and angry. I didn't understand then that I was burdening them with my unpleasant feelings. I see now that I was taking out my frustrations on my friends. In the end, they couldn't stand me, which left me alone to find other ways to rid myself of my pain.

Ira was having problems at work. He wasn't getting along with a woman with whom he was expected to collaborate, a conflict that had been going on for a year. Interestingly, Ira didn't feel as though *he* had a problem; his co-worker was the problem, and did she have problems! Talking with Ira's wife, Helene, I learned that he'd been "verbally abusing" her for a year by complaining and dumping his negativity on her. She had reached her limit; she didn't want to listen to him anymore, and she didn't want to be dumped on. Ira interpreted this as a breach of their marriage contract. He thought that it was her wifely duty to listen to his complaints and his negative talk. Helene saw herself sinking more deeply with each depressing story about Ira's "impossible" colleague. Ira had never admitted that he had a problem, and he found it all too easy to vent his frustrations on Helene. When I asked him about their sexual relations, he told me they'd lost all desire and ability to be intimate with one another. Little wonder: negative feelings breed negative results.

When anything like that happens to us, we need to look at ourselves, act to change our attitude, and move to a place of positive emotions. If one partner in a marriage or working relationship takes responsibility for integrating his or her feelings instead of re-circulating them, positive change will happen, at least for the person who takes the responsibility. Positive feelings in either will affect the other. Positive feelings create positive results.

Because Helene was no longer willing to listen to Ira complain, he was forced to find other ways to get rid of his emotional turmoil. If Ira had taken a good look at himself after discovering all the negative results in his life, he'd have been able to recognize that *he* had created the problems both at work and at home.

Surely, Ira didn't want these kinds of results in his life. One can safely say that the man did not tap into his emotional intelligence. Had he been able to feel his emotions fully, use what his feelings told him and manage his emotions, he could have created the outcome he wanted. Negative feelings breed negative results.

THOSE TROUBLESOME FEELINGS

Though we frequently hear, "use your head," "be sensible," and "think positively," the only real tool we have for changing our lives is our feelings. By integrating our negative feelings, the ones with which we least want to associate ourselves, we can find the energy to change, break free of our constraints, and create happy, meaningful lives. We simply need to learn how to channel this negativity and convert it into a positive state.

Positive feelings are easy to handle. They feel good, and they're usually not too complicated. Positive feelings are good for us and for the people around us. When we feel secure, loving, happy, self-confident, and calm, we have the energy to accomplish what we want, and we give to people just by being. We feel good about ourselves and close to others. Positive feelings influence our surroundings in a positive way.

Negative feelings are a different story. In a negative mood, we might feel sad, afraid, angry, frustrated, envious or irritated; we're uneasy, and don't feel pleasantly secure and

Nevertheless, it's essential that we acknowledge all this negativity, because that's how we begin turning it into a source of strength.

self-confident. Nevertheless, it's essential that we acknowledge all this negativity, because that's how we begin turning it into a source of strength. It's not wrong to have negative emotions; they simply are. My task is to show you how you can manage your negative feelings so you no longer feel powerless, guilt-ridden and afraid, and how you can use this knowledge to create a better life for yourself.

What we traditionally refer to as "upbringing" usually entails learning how to suppress and hide emotions. Although we think we can control our feelings and make them invisible, we all give out subliminal cues that enable people to know how we feel, and allow us to know how they feel, though we can't necessarily articulate these perceptions or understand them on a conscious level.

Life might be simpler without emotions, but it would also be dull. Everyone has ups and downs; sometimes we feel positive, other times negative. We're complicated creatures, carrying a bit of everything in us; no one is either all good or all bad. We embody a broad spectrum of feeling: love and hate, joy and sorrow, enthusiasm and indifference, magnanimity and pettiness, and every emotional state between. We can help ourselves by attaching no judgment to having any particular feeling. It's not "bad" to have negative feelings—they simply are. We need to remember, however, that negative feelings trigger negative results and influence others in negative ways.

How might you handle your difficult feelings? Basically, you have three choices: keep them inside, dump them onto your surroundings, or get them out without hurting those around you. The latter is what this book is all about; it's the emotionally intelligent way to handle your feelings. As the saying goes, "Dad beats mom. Mom beats me, and I beat the cat." There's some truth in this; what usually happens is that, first and foremost, Mom and Dad hurt themselves. Otherwise, they wouldn't feel the need to hurt someone else.

When our negative feelings are directed inward and have no outlet, they become self-destructive. Most of us have been taught that it's wrong to be angry, so, instead of releasing these feelings, we turn them on ourselves and bury them in the cellar of our subconscious mind. There they remain, doing harm, keeping us down, hurting us, making us passive and, in extreme cases, making us sick. Even when we recognize this, we continue to be angry with ourselves. Directing anger at ourselves keeps us from giving to others, because we can give no more or less to them than we can give to ourselves.

Modern psychology teaches that it's healthy to vent our feelings. It is important to speak our minds now and then, to clear the air and to let off steam. There are lots of ways to do that, but several of them are counterproductive and unacceptable.

Consider Arnie. When he was dissatisfied or irritated, either at home or at work, he seldom kept it inside. He believed that it was right and healthy to be direct and say exactly what he felt. Not surprisingly, then, there were many conflicts at home and in the office. Though Arnie felt relieved after speaking his mind, often those around him were shattered by his negativity. Understandably, they didn't hesitate to fire it all back at him.

Arnie was right in thinking that it's healthy to release one's negative feelings, but given all the paths up that mountain, there's no need to push everyone else into the abyss to get to the summit. Often, we're unaware of the other, more considerate alternatives. Most of us either release our negative feelings recklessly or bury them inside and act like they don't exist. Both paths breed conflict and unhappiness.

Let's get familiar with these negative feelings that cause us so much trouble and make us feel we're losing control and self-confidence. Before we can consider the possibilities of using negative feelings constructively, we need to examine their most difficult aspects. When we're angry, or annoyed, or full of self-pity and bitterness, and we keep these feelings inside, we become blocked. We cut ourselves off from critical information that could improve our lives. Believing that we see clearly, we are in fact blind. Those negative feelings block our intelligence and all the useful information concealed in our subconscious. We become separated from that most important, enlightening aspect of ourselves: knowing our inner voice.

Our culture teaches us that it's wrong to be angry, so we conform by suppressing our negative feelings instead of acknowledging them, feeling them fully, and then letting them go. We end up choking our growth and potential for change, and become prisoners in our own bodies. Only the truth within us can set us free, and our feelings are a vital part of that truth. We need to let them emerge if we are to grow and experience joy, insight and strength.

I used to think that I got my negativity from other people. Now I know that my emotions are no one else's but mine, and yours just as surely belong to you. We know that our positive feelings create a positive atmosphere, and negative feelings create a heavy, difficult environment around us. What we create is a direct result of what we feel and think, which is why our emotions are so important. Feelings help thoughts and thoughts help feeling.

"Emotions and thinking work together: emotions assist thinking, and thinking can be used to analyze emotion. Emotional intelligence is the ability to use your emotions to help you solve problems and live effective lives," says Dr. John Mayer.

We all know how it feels to 'get up on the wrong side of the bed.' The people on the subway seem bad-tempered; our colleagues seem inadequate; our boss is an idiot; and the children are impossible. If, on the other hand, we have just fallen in love again, the world takes on another hue. (Oh, what a beautiful morning; oh what a beautiful day.) Our reality is profoundly colored by our emotions.

We Carry Our Past with Us

Let's begin with a seemingly inane question: What's in a lemon? *Lemon juice,* you're probably thinking. The next question: Why does lemon juice come out of a lemon? Is it because you squeeze it, or is it because there's lemon juice inside the lemon? *Both,* you respond. This appears a rather simple thought, but let's develop it a bit further.

Imagine that you and I are lemons. Both our past and present are inside the lemon, whether happy or sad, calm or aggressive. From time to time we squeeze our lemon, or someone else does, and positive feelings come out. At other times a squeeze elicits negative feelings. We might agree that whatever comes out of my lemon belongs to me, and what comes out of your lemon belongs to you. Maybe we even agree that the juice was there from the start and that it was released because you or I or someone else squeezed it, or because of the *way* it got squeezed. The main point is that however it was set free, the juice (the feelings) belongs to the lemon (the person). If I do not accept the fact that my feelings come from within myself and are therefore my responsibility, I won't be able to create the life I want.

Now is the time to ask yourself whether you're willing to acknowledge that your feelings are your own and that they're entirely your responsibility. If my feelings had been a result of external influences, I couldn't have influenced my life in a constructive, positive way. When you give the responsibility for your emotions to others, you make yourself powerless. Choosing to accept that your feelings are yours alone is one of the most important choices you can make.

Choosing to accept that your feelings are yours alone is one of the most important choices you can make.

Once we accept our feelings, positive and negative, our challenge is determining what to do with them. Negative feelings are powerful; they deserve close attention because facing and managing them opens the way to happiness, closeness, success, strength, insight and clarity. Our true potential is hidden behind our negative feelings. By working through them we can uncover our gems, our true wisdom. By keeping them inside we stifle ourselves. It's essential to grasp this: If we can manage our negative feelings, work through them and get rid of them, we can find the treasures hidden beneath and move forward with our lives.

Susan's story illustrates this. As a child, Susan would run and hide whenever she felt pain or sadness. She'd clench her jaw and refuse to tell anyone what was bothering her. This was her coping mechanism, her way to survive the traumas she suffered in early childhood. When Susan was afraid, she'd simply hide behind the living room curtain and stay there until she felt the danger had passed. Throughout her childhood and into her adult life, this was how she met adversity. For all those years, she hoarded her unexpressed feelings of fear, aggression and anger, and they remained unresolved because she chose to not speak and share them with anyone.

Susan's father thought his daughter was very kind as a child, but also very stubborn. He favored her brother, who was outgoing and charming. Susan's mother, on the other hand, felt sorry for her, protected her and smothered her with love. In her adulthood, Susan's boyfriend treated her badly, so she resorted to her old coping mechanism: suffer in silence and "hide behind the living room curtain." Her feelings from the past emerged and combined with the pain of her present to cause severe depression.

When Susan wrote about her pain and sorrow until her hand became numb, her feelings began to come out. The more she dared to put them into words, the more she acknowledged them, and the stronger she became. This quiet struggle for survival took a long time. Through writing, Susan found the courage to speak her mind and end the relationship with her abusive boyfriend. She expressed in words all the painful feelings her father had induced in her, and she let him know exactly what she felt and where he stood in her eyes. The aggression that had mounted throughout her childhood was the driving force behind this liberating process, as is often the case. The cleansing process led to a more honest, loving and respectful relationship between Susan and her father.

Eventually, Susan grew happy. Cleansing her previous aggression liberated her inner resources. She went back to school and, for the first time, did extremely well. She had taken responsibility for working through all the negativity that had blocked her for so many years.

Despite her successes, there was still more for Susan to deal with. When her father passed away, she reverted to her old ways, taking refuge "behind the living room curtain." Her pain was so great that she felt as if she were fighting for her life again.

At such a point, you might want to give up and stop working through your feelings, but paradoxically, your joy has never been closer. The sorrow gives you one more opportunity to become more of yourself by moving through your feelings and integrating them so you become more whole, more ready for all the best life has to offer!

At that point Susan made an important choice. She chose to re-examine and face all the pain and fear that remained. She asked her brother, who loved her very much, to stop smothering her with love, as the memories of her mother's choking love were still very present in her mind. Even though her mother had been dead for twenty years, Susan held on to those memories as if the events had happened yesterday.

Sometimes we need a catalyst to bring out past wounds. By embracing the pain of the moment we can heal the pain of the past. Things began to really change when Susan decided to go through her negative feelings and integrate them; she began to feel stronger and clearer in her thinking. For the first time in her life, she felt confident about what she wanted. She decided to buy all of her brother's stock and to run their father's

If you identify and get rid of your negative feelings, you're already headed to a better life. ferryboat company. She felt fully alive, because she was realizing herself and her strengths.

We create our own world. If we decide not to live through our negative emotions and release them, our old ways of reacting and responding to life's events will persist, and we'll go on having the same experiences year after year. We are doomed to repeat our past, because, under the cloud of our negativity, we can only see the present and the future through the haze of our past. When we play out our negative feelings, we become able to neutralize our negative past and open the way to create a positive future.

How can we transform and neutralize negative feelings? There are several ways. Each requires that you delve into your feelings and allow yourself to sense them completely by putting them into words, regardless of how forbidden you've made them. When we put our feelings into words, we're on our way to removing blockages and seeing ourselves clearly. We can then become more calm and self-confident. We'll deal with this in detail in a later chapter, where you'll find practical exercises of proven value.

Inevitably, all of us meet with obstacles and adversity. The secret is to acknowledge this and deal effectively with our problems. This requires that we get accustomed to listening to our feelings. Train yourself to say, "I feel…" Now ask, "Where in my body does this feeling come from?" Feel it! What are the feelings that are hiding behind the initial feeling? What are they trying to tell you? Let yourself feel all of it, and then try to analyze what you feel. If you identify and get rid of your negative feelings, you're already headed to a better life.

When you channel negativity out of your feelings (preferably in a room by yourself), you can get in touch with your boundless positive emotions. We all have access to positive, loving feelings within after the negative ones have been sifted out. Not everyone believes this, however. Some fear that the world will discover the terrible truth about how bad they really are. We can be very hard on ourselves, believing that we're terrible creatures. In truth, you have an ocean of goodness and tenderness inside you, and you deserve to be loved by yourself and others.

When I coached Carl, the president of a large corporation, he told me, "When I'm sad now, I don't pull myself together the way I used to. Instead, I retreat to my office, close the door and let myself feel it. Before long, the sadness leaves me and I feel the positive energy again. Then I can listen to my heart and head again and fully trust my judgement."

Our challenge is to peel away the layers of sadness, fear, hurt and aggression so we can reach the love inside us. Instead of becoming anxious because you have been taught that negative feelings are ugly, remember that having negative feelings is perfectly normal. When you feel irritated, jealous, angry or petty, instead of criticizing yourself or suppressing or denying these feelings, take immediate action to integrate them and feel them fully. When you've identified your emotions and attached words to them, the negativity will find its way out, and you'll feel freer and stronger. It's that easy—and that difficult.

Alex, a director who attended one of my seminars, asked me why I gave so much attention to negative feelings. He preferred to focus on what was positive and to *be* positive. I remembered having been like Alex, so positive that I felt it was suffocating me. Thought and will alone can't cleanse us of our negativity, or integrate painful emotions so we grow and soar. It's not enough to "think positively." We can pull ourselves together by denying the darker side of our character, but this won't have lasting effects. We need to learn to manage our difficult feelings in ways that don't destroy us, but make us stronger, wiser, and more accepting and understanding of others and ourselves. Work through negative emotions, and they'll leave; try to forget them, and they'll live on. When you bring them out and become consciously aware of them, they can deepen your understanding of who you are and what resources you possess. This helps you tap your emotional intelligence, the kind of intelligence with more hope for creating a great life. Taking responsibility for cleansing yourself is a prerequisite for having something precious to give to others.

CONNECTING WITH YOUR FEELINGS

A life free of "troublesome" feelings could be simple, and cutting out contact with your feelings might appear to be a practical solution to many problems, but it would rob you of most of what makes life worthwhile. If we suppress our feelings we can't achieve real closeness with anyone. At best we get only the illusory closeness that casual sex, for example, might offer. To enjoy the wondrous experience of genuine closeness, we've got to heal the wounds that were previously inflicted on us, and we can't do that without contacting our feelings—the tools we need to get really close to people.

Without contacting your feelings, you can't tap your emotional intelligence. Your wisdom will lack depth.

Without contacting your feelings, you can't tap your emotional intelligence. Your wisdom will lack depth. You'll find it a struggle to achieve close relationships and be a good parent, leader, team member or effective employee.

Some people choose to divorce themselves from their feelings because perhaps, at some point, emotions got too painful to handle. Maybe they learned early that feelings were meant to be private and weren't appropriate to display. Others seem angry and openly aggressive all the time, while inside they yearn for love, tenderness and understanding.

Even if we close ourselves off from our emotions and have little contact with them, they live in our subconscious minds, and they influence our lives whether we realize it or not. To be out of touch with your feelings is to not know yourself.

Every emotion contains rich, important information about you and your past. Without contact with your feelings, you lose the potential to heal the wounds that you acquired long ago and that remain deep in your soul. To live a fuller and richer life and to connect with others, you need first to connect with and learn to know yourself. You achieve this by connecting with your emotions and allowing them to evolve. Feelings need an outlet, and you can provide it, giving your feelings and yourself a path to follow.

When we're out of touch with our feelings, we might find ourselves embroiled in conflicts we don't understand, resulting, perhaps, from signals we've given unintentionally. Our bodies speak an independent language that's rarely misleading. Body language can be very explicit. It often reveals the truth about our state of mind and heart. Even when we're separated from our emotions, our bodies can still tell the world the real story. We communicate our feelings to the world even if we're unaware of them. Similarly, we can consciously or unconsciously pick up and interpret the unintentional signals sent out by others.

Sometimes the separation between mind and emotions is so complete that it results in illness. Having no other outlet, feelings can manifest themselves psychosomatically and cause physical ailments. When you haven't taken your feelings seriously enough or given them a chance to be released, you might get a runny nose or itchy eyes. A common cold can signify that your body is "crying." Such colds often occur on a Friday after work, when your body finally gets a chance to rest and to weep.

Some of the people who come to my seminars are so cut off from their feelings that their bodies are completely rigid. Christian is a good example. I met him one summer while walking at the seaside. He walked toward me, his stature stiff and awkward. He told me he was unemployed and was trying to find another job. We chatted, and he seemed a fine, well-educated, resourceful young man. Yet, I couldn't help wondering what caused his rigidity. I wanted him to scream or cry a little to get out some of the feelings that created the stiffness. He seemed like an unexploded bomb, ready to go off any moment.

Christian asked me what my profession was. When I told him I conducted seminars in personal growth, leadership development and teamwork, he got very interested. He'd read some books about personal growth and leadership, but books alone are insufficient unless they're combined with exercises that awaken our feelings. Most of us have enough knowledge; what we need to really grow is the ability to process that knowledge through our feelings.

It was evident that Christian had never worked through his negative feelings and that they were holding him back. Such feelings tend to surface when we're challenged, such as by losing our job. Christian expended a great deal of energy keeping his negative feelings in check, smiling his frozen smile as if saying, "One has to be positive, damn it." Poor Christian was clearly close to breaking down.

Three months later, Christian decided to attend a seminar, where he sat bravely along with the other participants. Two weeks earlier, his wife had announced that she wanted a divorce. Composed and collected, seemingly devoid of emotion, they had discussed all the practical details. As with most discussions, Christian had approached this one as some kind of challenging academic problem.

Suddenly he asked if I could give an example of a feeling, so he could better understand what I was talking about. He was desperately trying to grasp these complicated issues. "If you pinch your arm," I explained, "you feel pain. It's physically painful. You have this kind of feeling inside you, but you're not in contact with it yet. In order for you to function more effectively, you need to become aware of these painful emotions. Otherwise, they'll keep standing in your way and making trouble for you. They are sabotaging your efforts to find a job and to pick up the pieces of your marriage."

After a while, I asked, "Was it hard being without a job?" Yes, indeed. Christian felt that he'd lost a lot of his self-esteem, and definitely felt less worthy now than when he had sat in a manager's seat. "Was it painful to lose your self-esteem?" Yes! He believed it was very painful (but he wasn't completely sure). For homework that day, I told him to go hit his mattress or his son's punching bag. The idea for him was to release some physical aggression to facilitate a connection with his anger.

Christian hit that bag until his knuckles were bloody. The next day he reported back to the group that his feelings were now beginning to flow: anger, and despair. His next homework assignment was to write down his feelings, his disappointments and grievances, anger and resentments, until he had nothing more to say. He wrote out all the feelings that had troubled him for so long. Afterward, he cried, and when he spoke with his wife, it was with genuine tenderness.

Going through the process that Christian went through can be very painful. Normally, one needs to repeat these exercises many times, but after each repetition one feels better. It's wise to ask for some help at the outset. Christian pounded his mattress for days, and wrote and cried. By emptying himself of his pain he came to a source of true strength. He also became clearer about how to handle himself and the divorce he was facing. At first, he hadn't taken his wife's wish to divorce him seriously, but ultimately they did separate, forcing him to confront the reality of their marriage.

Before Christian was able channel out his feelings, he was like a hunk of petrified wood. By the end of our work together, which took a long time, his life had become richer and more complete. Though he had lost his wife, he had found more of himself.

The end of Christian's story is atypical. In my experience, a husband and wife usually get closer through such a process. Perhaps Christian woke up too late to save his marriage, but not too late to save himself.

Each time we speak, Christian thanks me for bringing

When we're very busy we lose contact with our feelings; we overlook the signals they're trying to give us instead of taking the time to feel them. him closer to himself and to others. My response is always the same: "You did it yourself." Christian had the courage and willpower to work through his feelings. Without his persistent determination to do all the exercises, he wouldn't have gotten the results he achieved. He could have sought the help of a psychologist or psychiatrist, and though I recommended he do so, he chose to deal with his issues himself. Christian has gotten in touch with life by letting his feelings go. I thank him for choosing to work with himself and for his work with others. He has helped several other men by sharing his experience and insights with them. Clearly, his life is more meaningful than ever before. He continues to find more and more of himself, and the closer he gets to himself, the closer he'll become with others. Christian is a great example of someone who used his own difficulties as a steppingstone to growth. I know from experience that our problems can become our teachers and our lives become more meaningful when we view our trials and tribulations as a means to grow and live more fully.

Boy, How We Run!

We all want to create good lives for ourselves, but we run and run and run. When we're very busy we lose contact with our feelings; we overlook the signals they're trying to give us instead of taking the time to feel them. Our feelings carry intelligent messages and directions, but people on the run don't receive them.

The world demands a lot from us, but we put the heaviest demands on ourselves. If we want to tap into our emotional intelligence and benefit from it, we have to slow down and pay attention. It's just not smart to run with your head and heart working against you.

James is 'running' even when he's on the phone. The e-mails he sends are wildly incoherent. It's painful to be on the other end of the line with such a hurried person. His lack of sensitivity often shows up in his e-mail messages. He thinks he has a lot of emotional intelligence, and maybe he does, but what good does it do? We cannot tap into our emotional intelligence when we're running frantically. The ability to feel is the tool we need in order to tap our emotional intelligence.

When we're frantic, our conversations with other people feel like they're over the speed limit, and we're likely to think up ten new projects when we haven't finished the first one yet. I was impressed with such speed many years ago; now I see that it reduces our effectiveness at pursuing our goals. We need to slow down, and be aware and really in tune with our emotional intelligence and our inner voice to create a meaningful life. We can only hear and trust our inner voice if we calm down and pay attention.

Some years ago I coached Leo, a former corporate CEO. He had just lost his job, and was devastated. Finally, Leo had no more places to run. He reexamined his life from all angles, sorting out what was important to him. More and more, he began to live from the inside out. Leo has become one of the strongest leaders I know. He became president of a large international firm. He's loved, trusted and respected. He has confidence in his employees and, by giving training programs on the subject, has assured that everyone in his firm knows how to access their emotional intelligence. Leo has learned to share himself and his experiences openly; he's authentic, very empathetic, and communicates from his heart. He's very direct and dares to speak the truth. That makes some people uncomfortable, but Leo believes in being true to himself and to others.

It took Leo nearly a year to rebuild himself and bring out more of him than he had been aware of before. He paid the price. He has always been a wonderful person, but he'd never before brought it out in the open to such an extent. Before, he was running too hard to give himself time to be wise. Tapping your emotional intelligence is the same as gathering wisdom. Before Leo took on his new job as president, the company was losing money. Leo and his one thousand employees have turned it around and made it hugely profitable.

FIT FOR FIGHT

Erik gets up at 6:30 every morning—summer and winter—and puts on his training clothes. He walks for ten minutes, and then starts to run slowly. Twenty minutes later he's in the shower. There he asks himself, "How are you, Erik?" He senses his body. Does he have any stress or strain? If he does, he feels into it till it goes away. Then he decides what his feelings are telling him and what actions he wants to take. If he discovers that he's angry, he screams until he feels the anger is gone. After a peaceful breakfast, he's ready for work. At eight o'clock Erik is at work, physically and emotionally clean and prepared.

If unexpected events at work trigger his anger, he withdraws for a while to feel the anger and the hurt behind it, or he writes out his feelings till he's calm again. He checks into his feelings often to sense how the day is going and to see whether he's in touch. Erik can "safely" lead others then, because he's able to lead himself again.

All the executives I coach use tools to manage their emotions, tools that work for them daily, and help them pay frequent attention to their feelings and continually tap the power and direction of their emotional intelligence. We're all presidents of our own lives, and we're fully responsible for the results in our lives. To assure good results, maybe we'd better clean up and prepare for the day in more ways than one.

Closeness Is Something You Create

I know what most people long for, and I'm sure you know it too: closeness with people. I've asked thousands of people, and that's their answer. What strikes me, however, is how easily we lose sight of this goal. We tend to look for substitutes, like material goods or money. Sometimes we do things that are counterproductive and foolish, like blaming the people we long to be close to or express anger toward them.

While we're driven toward closeness, we don't necessarily want to be close to everyone, but there's one person I want to be close to all the time: myself.

While we're driven toward closeness, we don't necessarily want to be close to everyone, but there's one person I want to be close to all the time: myself. Being close to myself means that I feel a certain peace permeating my entire existence. I'm careful to remember that I can't achieve this peace as long as I'm feeling irritable, angry, aggressive, jealous, bitter, guilty, or self-pitying. To reiterate a point that was emphasized before, I can't feel close to anyone else unless I feel close to myself, and to achieve this closeness I have to cleanse myself of my negative emotions first.

The first time I felt a real sense of intimacy with my boyfriend, it was like nirvana, and I yearned for more of that blissful feeling of being completely at peace with myself. But it didn't return as I had expected, and I was annoyed because my boyfriend and I were unable to experience it again. My irritation dominated our interactions, preventing our closeness from returning. Eventually, I realized that the more I searched for that elusive feeling, the more aggravated I became when it didn't come, and the harder it was to achieve.

You can't hang on to irritation and feel close simultaneously; the feelings are mutually exclusive. Because I had longed for this feeling of closeness all of my life, I began working with my feelings. When I was irritated about something, someone, or myself, I wrote down everything I felt. After cleansing my system of all irritation I became calm, and the closeness I craved came naturally.

I spent a lot of time fuming about one thing or another, so there was plenty of writing and cleansing. After every session it became clearer that I had something to give, and I felt more convinced that giving is what is at life's core. We can have everything, but first we need to give everything. After we empty ourselves of all the trash that weighs so heavily on us, we can discover and bring out the best in ourselves. Only then can we feel the closeness we want with our loved ones. We might be tempted by the material world and consumer goods to fill our inner voids, but we know deep inside that there's no substitute for human connection, interaction and nearness. Above everything else on Earth, I want to feel close to myself and to others.

DIFFICULT PEOPLE

There was a time when it took very little to upset me. When people didn't behave as I expected them to, I concluded that *they* were to blame and needed to change. Slowly, it became *The way I feel* clear that *everyone* I knew bothered me in one *and think* way or another. My frustrating interactions with *influence my life* people rarely led me to question my own behav- *every moment.* ior, or suspect that I might be contributing to these difficult situations.

Later, I could laugh at the situation, having realized that the only thing that really needed changing was myself. I focused my efforts on that, and continue to work on it to this day. An awareness of all the contemporary research on emotional intelligence has motivated me even further. Every time I access my feelings—feel them fully—I know I'm using my emotional intelligence, using the information from my feelings to help me think. The way I feel and think influence my life every moment.

"Project Me" taught me an invaluable lesson: people are the way they are, and have the right to be that way. It's not my calling or responsibility to change them, but to learn to relate to them as they are. The more we understand each other, the better we can understand human nature and, ultimately, ourselves. Seeking to understand the lives of others will inevitably teach us more about ourselves. When we carefully observe our reactions to other people, we usually find that what we dislike in them reminds us of the things we struggle with in ourselves. By learning to accept ourselves as we are, we come closer to accepting others as they are.

During a transatlantic trip, I sat next to Henry, a frustrated manager of a pharmaceutical company. He had taken a few days off because he was fed up with his boss, whom he characterized as "a dictator." Henry confided that if he were younger, he would have quit his job, but as it stood, he felt trapped. Unfortunately, his 'vacation' had done him little good; he remained consumed with anger toward his boss, and thought of nothing else from the time he woke up till the time he went to bed.

Henry was distressed and exhausted. Ultimately, his quandary led us to a useful discussion of how to confront feelings of anger and powerlessness. Clearly, if Henry did nothing, his anger and bitterness would continue to break him down. Remember that negative feelings that remain inside you make you weak and create more negative consequences. Henry's negativity and anger could only worsen the animosity between his boss and him. He believed that the boss was unaware of his feelings, but our emotions are often apparent to the people around us. Many of us recognize one another's feelings and, consciously or subconsciously, we respond to those emotions. We need to acknowledge our own role in contributing to ongoing problems. Until we do, we continue to feel like powerless hostages to our anger. Henry's employer will feel that Henry is a threat to him and will "attack" somehow in response.

Sometimes, a difficult boss is a blessing in disguise. Henry's problems with his boss shed light on the issues that were already at play inside him. His professional struggles provided an opportunity to become aware of them and try to understand their origin. As we talked about Henry's past it occurred to me that his father had made all the rules at home, and that Henry was himself a bit of an authoritarian character.

Henry's confrontation with authority affected him far more deeply than he realized. How ironic that something so painful could be a catalyst for him to become freer, happier and better adjusted. Examining ourselves in the context of painful relationships helps us move beyond feeling threatened, hurt and angry, to self-discovery and enlightenment.

Many of the leaders I coach need to address authority issues. They need to confront the residual pain from unresolved relationships with childhood authority figures. Usually, it's their fathers, but it can also be other dominant figures from childhood. While the process can be lengthy, confronting and integrating these feelings neutralizes them, putting the leader back in the driver's seat, in charge, powerful and free to lead.

Once we understand ourselves honestly and lovingly, we can begin empowering ourselves by exerting self-control and self-discipline. We can find strength in shifting the responsibility for our interactions from other people to ourselves. By so doing, we can discover new, better ways to relate to people whom we find cold, discourteous or irritating, without focusing our energies on trying to change what's usually beyond our control anyway.

Learning to accept people who frustrate you takes discipline, but you can do it. We all know the expression "grin and bear it," and probably we've all had to. But what about having to relate to a difficult person over a long period of time in a setting that demands continual interaction? The grin-and-bear-it strategy becomes unworkable; we're forced to move beyond a quick fix and find practical approaches to foster more beneficial relationships.

One of the most important things we can do in relation to "difficult" people is to cleanse ourselves of all negativity toward them before we meet them again. The simple exercise of writing, in the form of a letter, everything (and I mean *everything*) you feel about someone provides an extraordinary release of anger and negativity. You might need to write a lot of unpleasant letters to someone (obviously, such letters are not intended to be sent) before the cleansing process is complete and you can meet him or her again without hostility.

Why is writing such letters so helpful? It helps us feel all of our emotions and, by doing that, integrate them. The next step is to read your letter and analyze what you wrote. This allows a more clear-thinking examination of your situation. Thoughts lead to words, which generate more thoughts. We come to see the other person differently and we learn to understand ourselves more deeply. By getting the thoughts and feelings "out" of us, we create opportunities for new interactions that aren't tainted by old animosity.

I can't stress enough that there's no better way to free yourself of painful emotions than to acknowledge them and move through them. Expressing them on paper is one way to do it, but there are several others. Taking responsibility can also mean asking for help, especially when confronting your feelings alone feels too difficult or overwhelming. You might want to seek help from a friend or a therapist. Regardless of where you go, recognizing that you need support is a sign of your determination and strength, not weakness.

We can all be privileged to serve as catalysts in other people's growth and development. To use an electrical metaphor, we can trigger positive or negative responses in others depending on the charge of our own batteries. Exciting possibilities arise when we recognize that influencing our own power source allows us to influence the lives of others. Take some time to consider how your thoughts and emotions are charged, and then think about how changing your frame of mind could affect your relationships. Look for ways to increase the positive aspects and decrease the negative ones, and then watch closely what happens in your relationships. You'll be amazed to see how much power you actually have at your disposal. The process of managing your feelings and the feelings of others happens in parallel. You have the power to create peace.

In summary:

❀ *You can't change your situation by expecting others to change.*

❀ *You need to see yourself clearly to improve your relationships.*

❀ *You have the power to improve any situation by managing your emotions.*

❀ *You need to acknowledge your contribution to ongoing problems.*

❀ *Every problem offers you an opportunity for personal growth.*

SETTING LIMITS

For many years I allowed myself to be treated badly, not knowing that I could influence the way people behaved toward me. I always felt like everyone else was in charge, and I was at the mercy of their benevolence or their cruelty. How empowering it was to realize that I could *choose* what I would accept, how I would let myself be treated. The key is setting limits.

Beth was married to Bernard, a man with psychopathic tendencies. When she came to my seminar, she was exhausted and very weak. When we were discussing how to discover our own strengths, I could sense that Beth was potentially strong and capable. When I told her so, she eyed me with surprise and disbelief.

A year and a half later, I met Beth on a ski trip. She looked radiant and was in the mood to talk. Standing straight-backed and strong, she told me that she had freed herself of her misery by writing down all the fury and anguish that had dominated her emotions. Realizing how much those emotions had hampered and weakened her, she committed her frustration and anger to paper. Feeling all her emotions, she had slowly but surely pulled herself together and set limits for her husband. While Bernard was intelligent and outwardly charming, in private he targeted Beth's weaknesses. His incessant criticism wore her down and made her a weak and submissive person whom he could control. When she got strong enough to confront him, Beth chose not to let Bernard treat her badly anymore. She decided to leave him, taking their daughter to protect her from his abuse as well.

You and I are responsible for how we let people treat us, because we have the sole responsibility for our lives.

You and I are responsible for how we let people treat us, because we have the sole responsibility for our lives. We need to determine our own boundaries and make it clear how we expect to be treated. We can't always control a situation, but we still have the right to choose how we relate to it; we need never ask for permission. Only you can set the limits for yourself. Remember that it's much easier when you've cleansed your feelings of negativity and aggression, because that gives you the strength to set limits.

It can be very difficult to set limits at your workplace. Several years ago I met Conrad, a bank executive who had been enjoying a great deal of professional growth and success. One vital area, however, was missing from his development: setting limits. Conrad loved his job. He had advanced very quickly from cashier to executive, but despite his success he felt empty and burnt out.

We discussed how he could take better care of himself and restore some of his previous energy. Finally, Conrad admitted that being ambitious wasn't always advantageous. He put so much into his job that at the end of the day he had nothing left to give to himself or anyone else. Not limiting what he was willing to do to further his career had taken a grave toll on

*When you're
unaware that
your own choices
can determine
the outcome of a
situation and you
wait for others to
choose for you,
you make
yourself into a
powerless victim.*

him. Now he had to face the fact and learn to make some concessions to a healthier life-style. When he had achieved a better balance between his personal and professional lives, he regained his energy and enthusiasm.

Learning to draw boundary lines requires that we first master our fear of not being liked and not meeting the expectations of spouse, child, friend or employer. Jill attended a seminar some years ago. She had two bosses and did everything she possibly could to live up to all their expectations. Jill was overworked to the point of exhaustion. I told her to sit in a particular chair, which she did immediately. Then I asked her to move to another chair, and she quickly obliged. The third time, she followed instructions and changed her seat again.

Later we discussed which of us had been in control. When she said she wasn't sure, I politely asked her to jump out the window (we were on the eighth floor and the window couldn't be opened). Jill got furious and ran into the hallway. After giving her a few minutes to think about the situation, I went looking for her. "I want to rip all the buttons off your tailored suit," she shouted angrily. That certainly wasn't hard to understand.

When the group reconvened, Jill described how it had felt to set a limit by choosing not to jump. At first she was very angry, but then she understood that it was her choice and not mine that had sent her hopping from chair to chair. It's easy to forget that it's our responsibility to set limits, even when a leader tells us to do things we do not want to do.

You are responsible for your own choices. You can always choose because *you* are responsible for your life. No one else knows what's best for you; you have to take care of yourself. Ultimately, you choose for yourself; no one can presume to choose for you. When you're unaware that your own choices can determine the outcome of a situation and you wait for others to choose for you, you make yourself into a powerless victim.

Several weeks after the seminar, Jill wrote to me. After giving a lot of thought to what had happened, she had concluded that she was the captain of her ship and was responsible for all the choices she made. Consequently, Jill had begun to evaluate her choices differently. Nothing was forcing her to continue working; no one was forcing her to do anything at all. She chose to do what she would do. Ultimately, Jill chose to move to another country, where she found another job. Previously, she'd been incapable of making such a big decision; she'd been too focused on the needs and expectations of others. Duty is a common excuse for not taking responsibility for our lives and doing what we believe is right for us.

It shouldn't surprise you to find people treating you with more respect when you refuse to be treated poorly. The more you allow yourself to be treated badly, the worse you'll be treated. It is important to understand that we ourselves create this vicious circle, especially when we let negativity build up inside us, which acts like a magnet for poor treatment. Holding on to negative feelings creates negative results.

It's amazing to see how people accept the limits you set. If you neglect to do so, they're free to set boundaries that might infringe on you. After decades of work on this issue, I still find it hard sometimes to set proper limits. The best I can do is to listen to my inner voice and choose what feels right. Your feelings are intelligent. They know what's right for you and what your limits should be. When you take the time to listen to that voice, it's loud and clear, and you can tell people where your limits are. Otherwise, how are they to know? You're the only one who knows; if you don't set your own limits, you're not taking responsibility for your own life.

The Futility of
Blaming Others—and Ourselves

After having the revelation that I'm entirely responsible for my life, I had to apply the knowledge to every part of it. I firmly believed that once I had, my efforts would bring me a sense of freedom, inner calm, and last but not least, a new kind of meaning. So, how could I apply my professional successes to my private life? If it's possible to influence others, how do I go about it? What more did I need to learn and understand? How could I avoid the common pitfalls so many of us fall into?

When I was a child, my family always looked for a scapegoat when something went wrong. Who forgot to lock the door? Who pushed over that plant? Who tracked the mud into the house? My family's way of 'solving' problems became mine in my adult life. I began to realize, however, that this was not only no solution, but also created more problems to deal with.

Clearly, if I wanted positive results I would have to stop looking for someone else to blame whenever something went wrong. Instead, I needed to identify the problem—not the person—and use my energy to find a practical solution. This approach brought different and very satisfying results, but it took time to implement this new way of thinking. It's important to remember that new ideas are exciting, but they require time and effort to take root and bear healthy fruit.

When things don't work out as you planned, it's easy to blame people or circumstances; it's much harder to find the real source of a problem. Having been unable to adopt this attitude in my private life, I felt powerless regarding the problems my husband and I were having. There was no doubt in my mind that he was at fault. I wasn't aware that people and relationships can grow in different directions, and I had firm opinions on what was right and wrong.

To try to save our marriage, we consulted a marriage

counselor, in whose presence we dished out our many mutual complaints. After trying to mediate our disputes, the counselor said to me, "Your husband is on railroad tracks, and you're on small, winding paths." He meant that my husband and I had embarked on different journeys. The question of blame was irrelevant; who was at fault made no difference. The point was that each of us had to follow the path that seemed right for us, and blaming one another wouldn't lead to a constructive outcome. Blaming never solves problems, in my situation or in any other.

If you want to create a more peaceful, meaningful life for yourself, stop blaming others and, most importantly, stop blaming yourself.

"My Conscience Is Bothering Me!"

Most people experience feeling guilty, but defining the core of a problem gets harder when we look for a culprit, someone else to blame. Most people are quick to blame themselves. It's been deeply impressed upon us that we're never as good as we "ought to" be and that we never accomplish as much as we "ought to." This attitude is so ingrained in our minds that we tend to be wary of anyone who doesn't seem to feel guilt. We assume that he or she doesn't understand responsibility and can't care very deeply about others.

Actually, we like our guilt. It's a handy excuse for avoiding what we don't want to do, while assuring the world that we're conscientious individuals. Sadly, we're so accustomed to carrying our guilt around with us that we're continually weighed down by "ought to's," and don't see the benefits we'd gain if we did away with guilt. Throwing away the burden of guilt means accepting ourselves as we are, and understanding that "ought to" is a creation of our imagination. Rather, we need to ask ourselves what *feels* right to do. What we call guilt or a bad conscience is a sure signal that we are in conflict with what we feel is the right thing to do. When we're quiet and at peace we know what's right for us to do.

The next time you feel guilty, feel it fully, because it will help you tap your emotional intelligence. The feeling of guilt carries a lot of valuable information that you need to know. What does feeling guilty tell you? Ask yourself whether it's because you aren't doing something you believe others expect you to do, or because you're doing something that goes against your fundamental values. As you train yourself to listen to your inner voice—the information from your head and heart—instead of following the imaginary or unexpressed expectations of others, you'll be less tempted to carry guilt, and do what your heart and head in combination tell you is right for you. That's using your emotional intelligence!

What happens when you have a guilty conscience? Just as all feelings are acceptable, there's nothing inherently wrong about feeling guilt. Let yourself feel it and feel it some more, staying in the feeling in an aware way. The fact that you can feel the pain of your guilt means that you're also capable of knowing why you feel that way.

Very little that's positive arises out of guilt-ridden actions. Consider what happens when you invite people to your party simply because you feel you "ought to," though you don't truly want them to come. You suffer through an evening of indifferent conversation while wishing they'd leave. Your conscience might be clear, but is it really worth it? It seems unfair to your unwanted guests to spend such an evening with you. Chances are, they came because they felt like they "ought to," and are suffering as much as you are. Where's the pleasure in a situation like that? Life is too short to ease your conscience that way.

As children, certain values are instilled in us: namely our parents' values. Often, when we experience guilt later in life, it's because we no longer accept those values. Because *you* are now in control of your life, you can reconsider those values from the past. You can examine and re-examine them until you can decide whether to keep or abandon them. Some might still feel right and good, while others now feel meaningless. This kind of reevaluation takes time and effort, especially considering how painful it can be to break away from our parents. After all, behind your adult self still lies a child's fear of rejection by mother or father.

Our feelings are never wrong; they exist as they are, and we're wise to pay full attention to what they can teach us. We can't choose them, but we can choose how we handle them. At my seminars, we talk a lot about guilt and bad conscience, often laughing at ourselves and at what makes us feel bad. What we don't laugh at, however, is the burden of guilt that weighs on some people so heavily that they can't enjoy love and happiness.

GUILT AND SELF-HATE

Years ago I met Alan, whose life story made an unforgettable impression on me. Twenty years prior to our meeting, he awoke in a hospital after a car accident and learned that his wife had been killed. Three days later, the police accused him of having caused the accident. He had been driving the car, but remembered nothing of the trip or the accident. He had spent the next twenty years feeling guilty, putting himself on trial for his wife's murder every day.

Through our work in the seminar, Alan came to understand that he had used twenty years' worth of energy keeping himself in a prison of self-reproach. He began to realize that neither he, nor his family, nor his work had benefited from his constant self-recrimination. After he had begun coming to terms with the consequences of his behavior—negativity, unhappiness, and nothing to give to those he loved—he asked to speak with me in private.

As we closed the door behind us Alan broke into tears. He cried and cried, letting out everything he'd kept inside until that moment. It was heartbreaking to see him share his pain. At that moment he decided to verbalize his feelings by expressing them in a letter. Also, he decided to visit his late wife's family so that he could share his grief and pain with them.

Alan chose to confront his emotions, and do all he possibly could to work through them. He needed to relieve himself of his guilt so he could have more to give to his new wife, his children, his friends and colleagues. He needed to feel, write and talk to rid himself of the pain and enable him to give something positive to himself and to others. Feeling guilty is often considered somehow noble, perhaps because we confuse it with taking responsibility for our actions. Until we've worked through our guilt and come to terms with our own values, we have little to give to the rest of world; this is what Alan finally understood.

If you hurt or kill someone, are you guilty? To try to answer this or any similar question, let's go back to the idea that each of us has responsibility for his or her life. If you willfully hurt another person, then you've got to take responsibility for that action. Even if you were insane at the moment, you still committed the crime. To expand on this thought, I'll tell you about Maria.

Maria became a mother at seventeen. Her child's father disappeared shortly after learning that Maria was pregnant, and her parents wouldn't help her with the baby. Maria loved her son from the moment he was born, and she never doubted her decision to have him. Nonetheless, she felt hopelessly alone with the responsibility for him.

After months of being awake most of the night with her crying baby, Maria was completely exhausted. One night when he just wouldn't stop screaming, she became uncontrollably furious. She picked the boy up and then hurled him back into his crib so hard that he stopped breathing. Had his head hit the side of the crib, the blow might have killed him. Maria managed to get her son breathing again, but she was in utter despair over what she had done. She wondered what kind of mother and person she was, who had nearly killed her own child. She wept and wept for what she had done and for fear that she might do it again.

Maria never did it again, and when she told me the story many years later, she also spoke about how she had worked through her anguish. It's an important lesson for all of us.

If we realize that what we did was wrong, but we work through to forgiving ourselves, we have more to give, including more compassion and empathy for other people.

In spite of my desperation, I instinctively understood that I had to find a way to forgive myself. I had to look at what I had done and recognize that it could never be undone, but at the same time I also had to look at the frightened, frustrated young girl who had done it. I needed to find a way to comfort and forgive her, because there was no one else to do it. I managed to say to myself that I had done a terrible thing, but I had not meant to. Had I continued to reproach myself and see myself as some kind of monster, I would have imprisoned myself in a labyrinth of guilt and blame, and increased the risk of repeating what I had done.

Becoming free of guilt doesn't mean refusing to take responsibility for our actions. On the contrary, it implies acknowledging responsibility and then working through our guilt feelings to reach understanding and forgiveness. Forgiving ourselves breaks the vicious circle in which violence and self-hatred breed more violence and self-hatred. We need to accept the responsibility of feeling our guilt so we can relieve it and then forgive ourselves. If we realize that what we did was wrong, but we work through to forgiving ourselves, we have more to give, including more compassion and empathy for other people. To feel compassion for the world, we need first to feel compassion for ourselves.

LETTING GO OF RESENTMENT—
THE HARDEST ONE OF ALL

The most important kind of resentment to get rid of is the one you most want to hold on to. Similarly, the most important people to stop resenting are the ones you resent most.

Carrying a grudge is the opposite of feeling and managing it. Carrying grudges is not emotionally intelligent, and affects your life in a negative way.

Why is it so important to let go of resentment? Your resentment builds a wall between yourself and the one you're angry with. The wall feels good and safe because it protects you from that person, but it accomplishes a destructive purpose: it blocks your innermost feelings and it cuts you off from your inner voice.

Letting go of resentment is how we can cleanse ourselves of our negativity. Many people misconstrue forgiveness for acceptance of wrongs committed against them. Forgiving means you're not carrying a grudge or feelings of anger or insult; your feelings toward someone don't have a negative charge.

What are the consequences of bearing a grudge? We feel like we're carrying a huge burden, masquerading as legitimate gripes. These continue to weigh on us every day that we choose not to feel them fully and thereby get rid of them. *Carrying* a grudge is the opposite of feeling and managing it. Carrying grudges is not emotionally intelligent, and affects your life in a negative way.

Sometimes we don't notice the connection between a quarrel at a given moment and a grudge that we later carry around. Whereas many endeavors give back the energy we put into them, and sometimes even more, a grudge only depletes our strengths without rewarding us.

Visualize your grudge as a weight that you carry all day long for years, when you get up in the morning, at work, at meetings, on your vacation, everywhere you go. Even when you're asleep, your grudge weighs on you, sometimes making you wake up tired and grumpy. Often, we carry resentment without seeing it as the source of our unhappiness and fatigue. We become so encumbered by our grudges that we can't give freely and generously to people. In other words, grudges prevent us from reaching our full potential.

It's unrealistic to believe that we won't feel annoyed with people, or have grudges. The challenge is what we decide to do with those feelings when we have them. We can't completely accept ourselves as long as we carry the burden of a grudge, because it acts as a symbol for all the resentment we've built up throughout our lives.

When we feel stagnant or weighed down, the only way we can forge ahead is by letting go of resentment. Instead, we keep blaming others for how they made us feel. Ironically, our resentment causes *us* pain, while our surroundings simply create opportunities for us to vent our feelings. These feelings belong to us, and to no one else, and they hurt us most deeply when they remain unacknowledged.

When coaching executives, I examine their thinking, because our thinking creates our lives. When I find that they harbor resentment, there's homework to do. Resentment needs to be felt and managed or leaders won't have the energy to create the career and life that they long for. It's easy to tell whether people have integrated and let go of their resentment, because resentment is a magnet for trouble. If someone is holding on to resentment, it doesn't take long before new problems surface.

Nate, a physical therapist, was telling me about some of his patients. It was clear to him that their lives would be better if they were willing to let go of their grudges. As he added it up: *sore muscles + stiff necks + grudging lives = sad, unhealthy people.*

When we feel sorry for ourselves, we risk another pitfall: we look for ways to rationalize our emotions, and we try to solicit support from others to justify our position. We've all heard and said, "She said this and that to me, and he did this that to

me, and isn't it terrible?" This game is called "Isn't it terrible
that . . . and don't you feel sorry for me?" We play it far too
often. Unlike other games, no one wins. Winners don't play
this game!

GETTING ON WITH IT

When Carla, a woman who had a seven-year-old son, attended
my seminar, she told me that the boy's father had run off the
minute he heard she was pregnant. She was on a crusade to
prove to this man that she could raise their son and manage
life on her own. Seven years later she remained just as determined to prove herself to him. It was easy to
understand that Carla had suffered a great deal
of pain, and because of it she was still very bitter.
To help her get back on her feet and out of the
trap she had walked into, I had to challenge many
of her motivations and assumptions.

I reminded her that pity strengthens the one that pities, while the one who is pitied is weakened.

Whether we admit it or not, we "enjoy" the attention of being pitied. It can be habit forming
and, like all habits, it can be very hard to give up. Carla had
been nursing her pain for more than seven years, so I asked
her how long she planned to continue coddling it and what
was her motivation for keeping the bitterness alive. Carla bravely
admitted that people felt sorry for her, and that if she no longer
focused on her husband's grave injustice she would lose that
attention. Her frankness and authenticity were admirable.

Later, I asked Carla to consider how much longer she wanted
to "enjoy" her pain. I recommended that she write (but not
send) some very candid and spiteful letters to her son's father
to help relieve the fury she felt toward him and thus diminish
her pain. Would Carla choose to work through her negative
feelings by committing them to paper, or choose to hold on to
her bitterness so people would continue feeling sorry for her?
I reminded her that pity strengthens the one that pities, while

the one who is pitied is weakened.

Three weeks later, Carla had already relieved much of her anger by putting it on paper. She confessed to having felt angry not only with her child's father, but also with me. She was proud of herself for having confronted her anger with the intention of letting go of it instead of wallowing in it. She told me she felt tremendous relief, and thanked me for not "yessing" her through this process, which had forced her to acknowledge some difficult and painful aspects of her life. Who we are and where we are is determined by our own choices.

Carla's story supports my belief that people who want to get on with their lives must first weed out their grudges, their bitterness and resentment, and work through the feelings that have given them a destructive kind of nourishment. Some people live their entire lives on that kind of "fuel"—no wonder their lives are void of love and happiness.

The Scary Thing about Being Right

After suffering traumatic experiences, many people build around them a thick-walled castle of anger and resentment. They've been hurt and want to make sure that no one gets the chance to hurt them again. The problem is, it gets very lonely inside such a castle—another reason why it's so important to acknowledge our grudges. Integrating your painful feelings by feeling where in your body they are, sensing what other kinds of feelings there are in that part of the body, resting into the feeling and staying there for a while is like removing a wall of resentment stone by stone. If you don't, you could be imprisoned for life. If you put your mind and heart to it, you can put your anger and resentment behind you. Your life will get better and you won't feel lonely. You might choose to be alone, but you won't be lonely.

Everyone has resentments to leave behind. The million-dollar question is, "Do you want to be right, or do you want to be happy?" One may exclude the other. Often, in order to be happy, you need to stop continually wanting to be right. The loner's gravestone reads, "I WAS RIGHT. I DIDN'T HAVE LOVE, CLOSENESS, FREEDOM OR HAPPINESS, BUT I WAS RIGHT, DAMN IT!" Take a while to reflect on this. We all enjoy being right, but we need to consider the cost.

Inside each of us is a little child who deserves to be happy and loved. Life provides us ample opportunities to love others and ourselves, and giving up resentment opens the door to these opportunities. Take a moment to ask yourself, "What's the hardest thing for me to stop resenting? How great is the pain I'm clinging to? Do I want to hold on to it, or would I rather let it go?" The good news is, if you feel it, you've got a chance to transform it. Remember that many people can't feel at a conscious level, but their feelings do a lot of damage, reflected in poor relationships and empty lives. If you can feel, you can integrate your feelings by staying in them for a while and asking yourself what they're about and what they tell you. When you do, you're tapping you emotional intelligence, making your head feel smarter and your heart feel lighter.

I encourage you to feel your pain and bring it out into the open. Even when it feels like it might be too much, keep going, because you're probably on the verge of a breakthrough. Consider whether you have the strength to continue carrying your anguish, or whether you want to free yourself of it once and for all. When you're sure you've felt the depths of your pain, you're ready to give it up.

Giving up resentment is giving ourselves a gift of freedom. If we don't offer ourselves this gift, we remain chained to the lingering sorrow of our past, recreating again and again the same painful conflicts in different disguises. With the channel to the love inside us blocked, we hold back from giving to ourselves and to the people we love. We do the same in our careers as well, and when we don't give, we don't receive.

Hal, one of the leaders I coach, called to tell me about having

visited the parent company and the head of the *Holding on to*
multinational conglomerate business he works for. *resentment gives*
A lot had happened as a result of Hal's coaching: *those we resent*
for one thing, his sales had doubled. But what he *power over us,*
allowing them to
wanted to share with me was the enormous calm *take even more*
and confidence he felt during his time with "the *out of us than*
big boss." Only months ago he had felt anxious *they already*
and somewhat inferior. Now he felt strong, confi- *have.*
dent and relaxed. He was really happy and relieved,
and said that he knew it was because he had given up resentment toward authority figures. Hal had been aware of his feelings
and managed them easily while the meeting was going on. He
had mastered the art of tapping his emotional intelligence. He
listened to his head and his heart as the discussions unfolded.
He created trust, and connected well not only with his boss but
with all of his managers. He ended our conversation by saying
that the payoff for the work he had done and the tools he acquired through personal coaching were greater that he had been
able to imagine.

Holding on to resentment gives those we resent power over
us, allowing them to take even more out of us than they already have. You can give up your resentment if you choose to.
You deserve to be happy in your relationships, but you can
only do it if you're willing to give up your resentment. There's
no other way, no shortcut to feeling good.

Take the time to cleanse the negativity from your mind and
heart, and your life will be much happier and more fulfilling.
No one can give up resentment until all their negativity has
found some means of expression. Giving up resentment isn't
the same as swallowing your negative feelings; rather it means
living through them, integrating them and feeling them, and
then they "evaporate." Find the method that works best for
you, and don't wait until you're 'at war' with someone to start
this process. Succeeding at this will be one of your greatest
accomplishments, so build a reward system into your method.

Buy yourself a small gift, write yourself an admiring letter, take time for a walk in the sun, or go have some fun with friends—whatever you feel is an appropriate reward. (Try not to reward yourself by doing things that aren't healthy for you, even if they feel good.) Giving up resentment is hard, but going through life carrying it with you is much harder.

FORGIVING THE UNFORGIVABLE

At one of my seminars, Laura told me that her father had sexually abused her every day from the time she was four years old. At the age of eleven Laura was stricken with epilepsy, because, she claimed, she had to escape from her father's abuse. As an adult she wanted to live a happy, productive life, but she understood that she couldn't do this as long as she continued to dwell on the terrible wrongs her father had committed against her. Laura spent years in therapy with a psychologist in hopes that treatment would help her let go of the pain and rage that were destroying her and everything that was important to her. She realized, however, that she needed several other kinds of help and support to pull her out of the emotional quicksand she was sinking into.

We can't lead a "good" life and hate at the same time. Unless we cleanse and neutralize our negativity, we just go on creating more negativity. To reiterate, letting go of resentment doesn't mean accepting the wrongs done to us; it means becoming free of them. Painful feelings and negative energy can serve as catalysts for change. Life can become so unbearable that our only choice is to change or suffer. When I met Laura, she had already gotten rid of much of her hatred and contempt, and she was ready to let go of her remaining feelings of resentment. She was on the verge of being free.

Laura's story made such an impression on me that I relate it in many seminars. If she, who had experienced the worst kind of abuse and injustice imaginable, could forgive her father, then we can forgive much lesser transgressions.

Hearing this story, many people ask why Laura should forgive her father, when he was so wrong and she so innocent and
vulnerable. I respond that forgiving was the only way Laura
could become truly happy. Without letting go of the pain and
anger from her past, without fully feeling and integrating those
feelings, she would have ensured herself a life of despair. People
who can't grasp this connection can spend their entire lives
stuck in the past.

In connection with a celebration of the fiftieth anniversary
of the liberation of Auschwitz, a Jewish woman told her story
on TV. Ida was only nine when she was put into a concentration camp where she ultimately lost her entire family. Her life
was spared only because she had been made a guinea pig for
Nazi medical experiments. The doctor who had done his "research" on her was now dead, but Ida had subsequently met
and spoken with another doctor who had perpetrated similar
atrocities in a different concentration camp.

The two of them sat together on camera. The doctor explained that he hadn't been strong enough to say no at the
time, because he had a wife and child to support, and he feared
losing his license to practice. Ida gave an account of the pain
she experienced and the resentment she carried after all she
had been subjected to in the camp. She had demanded to meet
one of the doctors who had worked in Auschwitz; she wanted
him to give her a written declaration admitting and regretting
his awful acts of abuse. Only then would she be able to forgive.
"It was as if all my pain was taken from me, and I was at peace,"
she said.

Ida chose to forgive so she could live in peace. Some of us
maintain that such gruesome acts are unforgivable. Recall the
message of many survivors of Nazi terror: "We must forgive,
but never forget." Again, to forgive and let go is not to accept
the wrong that was done. It's crucial to understand the difference to be able to work through the pain, to become free and

go on living. We need to understand, however, that we can forgive only on our own behalf, and that we can't put ourselves in another person's place. We need to respect those who are unable to let go of their resentment. It's a process that takes time; for some people a lifetime might not be enough.

The consequences of our choices are reflected in the way we live. We *are* the result of our choices. Others don't make choices for us unless we choose to let them. Recognize that not to choose is also a choice, perhaps the most dangerous choice of all.

The Right to Make Mistakes

It's human to make mistakes; no one can avoid it. Still, many people find it hard to accept that errors are unavoidable and that we have the right to make mistakes. Mistakes can be embarrassing and painful, and can taint our self-image. Some mistakes can have devastating consequences, not only in our own lives but in others' as well. The question isn't whether we'll make mistakes, but how we relate to and deal with the mistakes we'll inevitably make.

Many successful companies acknowledge the human propensity for error. Their philosophy is that if you haven't made any mistakes, you haven't taken any chances. One company I worked with actually awarded prizes to the employees who made the most mistakes, recognizing a strong correlation between mistakes, creativity and initiative. After all, how many blunders do you think Edison made before he built a functioning light bulb? Three thousand!

In some situations, errors are simply unacceptable. There's a big difference between a waiter who spills gravy on a customer's new dress and a surgeon who forgets a scalpel in a patient's abdomen. Where human life is concerned, special precautions must be taken to reduce the possibility of error. Surgeons don't operate alone, someone in addition to the pharmacist checks the prescription, and there are always two pilots on a plane.

The range of response to other people's mistakes varies tremendously. When you dial a wrong number, some people are polite and friendly; others become very irritated. We have the power to choose how to handle our own mistakes and those of others. Instead of seeing mistakes as evidence of incompetence and sloppiness, try to see them as an integral part of life, to be embraced in a kindly way. When people make mistakes, treat them the way you'd want them to treat you.

The first time an adult admitted to me that he had blundered was when a friend of mine was two hours late to meet me. I was furious. "I made a mistake and I'm so sorry," he said in a disarming way. I was dumbfounded. There was nothing more to say. My anger melted. He had completely defused the situation, and I could no longer nourish resentment. That very simple interaction was in fact my most important lesson in how to calm a situation by admitting an error and allowing myself to proceed.

Eventually, the day arrived when I made the mistake that I had dreaded making for years: I forgot an important meeting. To add insult to injury, I was the one who'd invited two directors to lunch. When they arrived at the restaurant on time, I was in my cabin in the mountains, peacefully reading a book. Only when the phone rang did I remember my commitment. There and then I acknowledged my feelings of shame, felt them, and went on with life in an emotionally intelligent way.

Later, reflecting on what had happened, I understood the reason for my forgetfulness, but there was no point in making excuses. While I regretted my error deeply, I still believed that we all have the right to make mistakes—consoling at that moment. There was no undoing what was already done, so the challenge was to figure out how best to deal with it. First, I sent flowers to both of them, with a note saying that I was very sorry for my blunder. Then I took some time to think about how to avoid repeating the same mistake. Fortunately, I was

If we can forgive ourselves, we can forgive others for their mistakes. dealing with mature people who understood that mistakes happen to everyone. I know one of them well; her forgiving attitude brought us even closer, and I saw more clearly what she was really like.

Years ago such a scenario would have caused me great anxiety. I was much stricter with myself then. After a slip-up like that, my feelings would have been quite different: "Ugh! How could you have done something so stupid, Randi? You're really an idiot!" After berating myself I would have made elaborate excuses to the people involved, expecting them to understand. Afterward, I would have blamed myself for the rest of the day—and the next. Would anyone have benefited from that? No. Also, I would have worried about what those people thought of me, though none of us can control other people's responses. They react to mistakes in their own way, and that's their right. In this instance I was lucky. Perhaps in your experience people got angry and distanced themselves from you because of your mistakes. We can't know how people will react, but we can know how we want to deal with our own mistakes.

When we make mistakes, as we inevitably will, it's best to acknowledge them and move forward. If we allow frustration and embarrassment to be our dominant emotions, we pay too high a price. Self-inflicted punishment isn't the best teacher; real growth occurs when we admit our mistakes and forgive ourselves for making them. Endless self-recrimination benefits no one. If we can forgive ourselves, we can forgive others for their mistakes. Blundering occasionally helps us develop as human beings and be more accepting and forgiving. I'm sure you empathize with people who make the same mistakes you once made. Or have you forgotten what it was like to be you at that point?

"We learn from our own mistakes" has become an old adage because it holds true. Think about how you relate to your mistakes. We can't lead error-free lives; we need to accept mistakes as part of life. That doesn't mean we shouldn't try to improve ourselves. On the contrary, our mistakes are important catalysts for analysis and self-improvement.

Looking for Praise

Everyone likes compliments; I'm no exception. I used to be a compliment addict, utterly dependent upon approval. Even when I got compliments, I felt they came too late and weren't exactly what I wanted. I believed that praise would give me the self-confidence I lacked. It cost me a great deal to cure myself of this ailment, but I realized in the end that the approval I sought from others was a poor substitute for trusting my own judgment.

Why do we look for substitutes for our own inner wisdom? Simply put, there seem to be two ways to lead your life: rely on your inner voice, or depend on the external world and its opinion of you. We all live a combination of the two, but when we tap our emotional intelligence we live from the inside out. When we don't, we live from the outside in. When we feel empty and lack inner calm and self-confidence, external compliments can raise our spirits. But focusing too much on them decreases our chances of discovering our true inner qualities and having our inner voice direct our lives. John's story illustrates this.

John was the vice president of a large corporation that hit some rough times and was considering a layoff of 200 employees to survive. For over a year, John had been vying for a big contract that Peter, the company president, was convinced they couldn't get. But John never gave up, and eventually landed the contract. He was bursting with pride when he went into Peter's office to share the news.

A man of few words, Peter wasn't in the habit of handing out compliments. His reaction to John's news was simply, "Good." John had dreamed of this moment for a long time, imagining that his boss would exclaim something like, "Congratulations!

There are risks associated with continual searching for approval and being dependent on compliments, but there's no risk involved in giving compliments.

You've saved this company. I can't thank you enough!" But Peter didn't say that. Maybe he should have, but there's no use focusing on 'ought to'—we must simply accept what Peter said.

For three months, John was consumed with anger over his disappointment at the lack of presidential appreciation, and carried that hostility around with him every day. It was affecting his work and his home life dramatically. Finally, his wife exploded, "Deal with your anger and be done with it—I can't stand listening to this anymore."

Everyone knows how easy it is to fall into this kind of trap. We'd all like to change our bosses into what we think they "ought to" be. At best, we can influence people to a modest extent, but we can't really change them. Through our sessions, John was eventually able to break the circle of anger and silent recrimination. Instead of concentrating on his disappointment and sadness over Peter's reaction, he was able to focus on his own well-earned pride and satisfaction. After all, he had achieved something important. In the end, John's approving opinion of himself proved sufficient. Only after dealing with his pain could he accept his own compliments for making the great sale.

By believing firmly in ourselves and trusting our own judgment, we can find peace even if others can't express their approval. Our inner voice is far more powerful than anything we receive from the world outside.

There are risks associated with continual searching for approval and being dependent on compliments, but there's no risk involved in *giving* compliments. We're all human, and even for those who know and nurture their inner voice, a compliment can never hurt. When a job is done right, well-deserved appreciation is appropriate and encouraging. Too many leaders are reluctant and stingy about praising their collaborators. After all, even leaders are not immune to praise.

2

GETTING YOURSELF
WHERE YOU WANT TO GO

———◆———

PROBLEM SOLVING

It's trendy today to say that there are no problems, only "challenges." I strongly disagree. Of course, we all have problems; it's foolish to believe otherwise. We'll have to contend with difficulties as long as we live; that's what life is about—confronting our problems, defining them and finding solutions. Along the way, people might try to tell you that your problems aren't real. Good bosses listen to their co-workers and don't ignore their problems. The appropriate response is to ask, "Have you been able to define what the real problem is?"

It's very frustrating when a husband and wife have no interest in listening to one another's troubles, and it's infuriating if one tells the other, "Your problems aren't real." Problems are very real to those who feel they have them. Obviously, what you perceive to be a problem, *is* a problem. Similarly, if your partner feels that he or she has a problem, it *is* a problem and it needs to be taken seriously.

As social creatures, we tend to minimize the importance of problems. Our mothers have so often said, "Let's not fight now, when we're having such a nice time!" (It's usually a mother who assumes the role of peacemaker.) If we're afraid to admit that we have problems, and choose to maintain a façade of peace instead of delving into them, we risk growing farther apart.

Pretending a problem doesn't exist just makes it grow bigger and more destructive. I learned this long ago from my mentor and leadership consultant, LeRoy Malouf, who said, "If you ignore the problems and just try to build on the positive, the positive won't grow, but the problems will." His wise words have changed and healed organizations and relationships. When you deny the problems in an organization, it will go bankrupt. If you deny the problems in a relationship, it will go 'bankrupt.'

When the Iron Curtain fell, all the problems in the communist countries became evident. Rulers in the former Soviet Union had systematically denied to their countrymen and to the rest of the world that they had serious difficulties. Perhaps they believed that admitting the unpleasant truth might dispel the myth that communism was the ideal system. Their refusal to admit the existence of problems, and their failure to try to correct them, caused the inevitable collapse of the system.

In my seminars, we often use stones to represent our problems. (No one can accuse us of dealing with imaginary problems!) Stones of various shapes and sizes are placed on the table in front of each participant. The size of each stone is meant to reflect the magnitude of the problem.

Once, a waitress who was serving us coffee asked if we were geologists. "The stones represent our problems," I replied. She got it immediately, and related how she struggled with her problems. "I take them to bed with me at night. I have so many that there's not enough room for me in the bed, and I can't fall asleep. I'm up making coffee by four o'clock every morning, and I'm tired even before I start working." I suggested that she try using stones to define and sort out her problems so she could deal with them one at a time. Several months later, the waitress approached me enthusiastically and said, "I'm sleeping much better now!"

Many people don't realize that a problem that's been defined and understood is already halfway solved. Problems you haven't identified and analyzed will stay unsolved.

Many people don't realize that a problem that's been defined and understood is already halfway solved. Problems you haven't identified and analyzed will stay unsolved. When you take time to understand what the real problem is, you begin to see how to tackle it. The ultimate challenge is solving the problem, but first you need to know what the problem really is.

Do you know the difference between a challenge and a problem? A challenge might seem awesome, but it brings out new strength in you when you decide take it on. Consider what happens when you start a new job. You're facing a number of unfamiliar situations, and you feel nervous, but you're also excited. You want to succeed in this new endeavor, and you look forward to making the necessary effort. A problem, on the other hand, tends to make you feel overwhelmed, weighed down as if you had a heavy stone in your stomach. Analyzing the problem enables you to transform it into a challenge. The definition is clear, and you feel energized.

Your emotional intelligence is an amazing problem-solving tool. Researchers Dr. John Mayer and Dr. Peter Salovey tell us that an accurate understanding of our emotions makes us better at problem solving. As an executive coach I know that what they're saying is true.

So, what's your problem? What's your *real* problem? At our seminars we question one participant at a time, after he or she has presented a particular problem. We agree beforehand to direct all our attention to one person's problem. Also, we promise not to give any advice concerning the problem. We ask the questions, and the participant answers them. Hoping to uncover the core issues, I ask at critical moments, "What do you feel is the problem?" Experience has taught me that what people originally believe was their problem was not in fact the underlying difficulty. It's amazing to watch how a participant's problem can change content through a dialogue that begins as simply as:

"I have a problem at work."
"What's the problem?"
"I'm bored and I feel very tired."

Sometimes the participant ends up choosing to make some changes at work; another discovers that the real problem is in his or her marriage, and yet another realizes that he or she needs to change professions entirely. We ask questions until the participant is satisfied, having completely understood the problem by feeling it and defining it until he knows that *that* is the real problem, because it makes sense and, most importantly, because it feels right. Clearly, what's on the label isn't always what's inside the bottle. Every problem has elements of emotion in it; that's what makes it a problem. Feeling the problem integrates your emotions and makes the problem feel lighter. When it's fully defined and felt, you've got a challenge!

If we had no problems and no challenges, we'd have little to drive us forward, and life could get exceedingly boring. There's real excitement in challenge—admittedly, sometimes too much excitement! My life, perhaps like yours, has been full of problems and challenges. With time, it's become easier to accept this reality, not because my problems have become simpler, but because I've learned to enjoy the game of defining, feeling and solving them. It's exciting, because I'm moving forward every time, and I feel like a bird soaring in the sky.

WE ARE RESPONSIBLE FOR
SOLVING OUR OWN PROBLEMS

I met a Swedish business manager on a plane several years ago. We discussed the value of seminars on management development. He had attended many, and felt that he'd usually gotten his money's worth. I asked, "What was the most important lesson you learned in these seminars?" He replied, "I learned that it's my responsibility to deal with my own problems. This realization has directly contributed to my success in business and in my personal life. Too often, people sit and wait for someone else to solve their problems."

The great mistake in waiting for others to solve your problems is that what you consider a problem might not be a problem to someone else. Our problems are real to us if we feel them to be, and our responsibility for solving them is equally real. At my seminars, it's surprising to see how many people with really serious problems deny having any at all. They don't understand that we need to understand and confront our problems to move ahead with our lives.

Sometimes our problems are blessings in disguise. They're like surprise packages: when we take off the wrapping and see what's inside, we learn something new that we can build upon. Try to see your problems as friends who'll carry you to your next challenge, a challenge that will make you fly.

When you know what your problem or challenge is, and you've accepted the responsibility for doing something about it, the question is "What do I want to do about it?" You have three options:

1. *Do something about it now. Tackle the problem. Apply
   the tools at your disposal and find a solution.*

2. *Bury it.*
If you pick this option, you need to choose a date when you're

going to work on it again. If you put off dealing with a problem, it stays in your subconscious mind, where you continue to work on it. By working through it on a conscious level, you make it easier on your subconscious, because you've put your difficulties into words and defined your problem. Despite what many people believe, we can control our thinking. When you analyze a problem actively, you're actually exercising control of your thoughts, which is a sure way to help yourself.

3.Throw the problem away if it belongs to someone else.

Often, people discover that they've been carrying around someone else's problem. This can happen when you take responsibility for someone else's life, which is forbidden territory. Perhaps you counseled a friend or relative who then chooses not to follow your advice. You might feel responsible for this person and spend lots of time and energy worrying, because he or she has chosen to do things differently. This, however, is not really a question of your responsibility. When you offer opinions, the recipients have the right to choose what to do; ultimately, their lives are their own responsibility. You don't necessarily know what's right for someone else. The best you can do is to ask questions; the burden of answering them isn't yours.

As an executive coach, I'm careful to avoid thinking that I have the answers to everyone else's problems. I ask questions from every possible angle until my clients find their own answers.

Sometimes, as we try to work through our problems, we ask questions like "Why am I having to deal with this?" This is a useless exercise until we turn it into "*How* am I going to deal with this?" When you stop focusing on why you have problems, and take responsibility for feeling, defining and solving them, you might need help from others: perhaps the advice of a doctor, or a psychologist, or a lawyer. We all need good advisors and discussion partners, sometimes outside our immediate circle of family and friends. Nonetheless, it's important that you never give your decision-making power to someone else.

Your Goal, Your Driving Force

If you had only one year left to live, what would you do? Assume that you have enough money to live on, and you're still healthy enough to enjoy it. Give yourself some time to contemplate these questions:

❀ *Would you continue working for the same company or in the same field?*

❀ *With whom would you choose to spend your time?*

❀ *Would you spend more time alone or with others than you do now?*

❀ *Would you feel the need to ask forgiveness for anything you've done?*

❀ *Do you want to forgive anyone?*

❀ *Would you feel a desire to talk things over with anyone?*

❀ *Do you feel as close to people as you would like?*

❀*How much time would you devote to your hobbies?*

❀ *Do you know what makes you happiest?*

❀ *Whom do you want to make happy in your last year of life?*

❀ *Which of your previously unfulfilled needs would you like to fulfill?*

❀ *Have you thought about how to fulfill these needs?*

❀ *Do you want to continue living with your current partner?*

❀ *Do you want to go on living in the same place?*

❀ *What have you always dreamed of doing but haven't yet done?*

We don't know what tomorrow will bring, so we need to live this very moment the way we genuinely want to. Now—right now—is all we have.

If the difference between your present life and your hypothetical life with only a year to live is vast, it's important to start changing your priorities. We don't know what tomorrow will bring, so we need to live this very moment the way we genuinely want to. Now—right now—is all we have. Many people are unconcerned with goals, presumably because they don't understand the joy and energy that arises from knowing what you want out of life.

What we are and where we are is a result of our previous thoughts and decisions. This became evident to me during a very difficult period in my life. It was painful to admit that I had caused the difficulties I found myself in. Had I chosen to believe that someone else had caused my troubles, the situation would have been far more difficult, because I would then have felt powerless to change my life for the better. The message was clear: I alone had made my life into the mess it was by following my own thoughts and priorities.

When I became aware of the potential to influence my life by discovering and focusing on what was truly important to me, I felt enormously uplifted. I became increasingly aware of concentrating on the thoughts that would take me in the direction I wanted to go. I wasn't playing the role of victim anymore; I had taken control of my choices and therefore of my life. My life became an exciting adventure when I accepted the fact that I created it. Choosing to believe that external circumstances could dictate what happens to me would have been surrendering control of my destiny; giving my power to an impersonal and often-uncaring world. Instead, I chose to influence my life and embrace the power to make decisions that were mine and mine alone. I had to ask myself the difficult questions about what I really wanted out of life, and promise to answer them with complete honesty. Regardless of where you are at the present moment, asking these questions and answering them truthfully from your heart will set you free.

Your Thoughts Are Free

Viktor E. Frankl's book, *Man's Search for Meaning*, made a great impression upon me. In it, the Jewish psychologist recounts his experiences in a concentration camp during World War II. The most fascinating aspect of his account is his explanation of how he survived the most horrific circumstances by understanding that no one could take away his freedom of thought. Frankl maintained that the prison guards could have done whatever they wanted, and though he remained a prisoner, his inner self would always be free. He always had the freedom to think whatever he wanted to think; a freedom no one could take from him. I recommend this book highly to those of you who are seeking greater freedom of thought, especially those who find themselves in difficult or painful situations.

Frankl also writes about the importance of having a goal, something to look forward to, a reason to survive in the camp. For some it was reunion with relatives after the war, or revenge on the prison guards. Goals that are important to us give us power to live.

I reached a new level of understanding of the importance of goals and thoughts during the first "Ski for Light" competition in the United States. I was to escort Jean Emere. Thirty-two years old, he had previously been on France's downhill ski team with the Olympic gold medallist, Jean-Claude Killy, but Jean Emere was now blind. We were to train together for the competition set to take place one week later, in which seventy-two blind cross-country skiers would participate.

My job was to ski the track next to Jean and to tell him the length of the downward slopes and whether the track veered left or right. On the first day of training, after skiing a couple of miles, I heard a terrible sound from Jean's lungs, as if he couldn't breathe. Stopping him, I said, "You can't go on in this condition. I'm so worried hearing you breathe like that."

"You don't understand what this is about," he responded. "I'm a diabetic, and I haven't much time to live. I'm determined to win next week!" There was no misunderstanding the man; he knew what he wanted. My only question then was whether his shortness of breath was connected with his diabetes. "No," he replied. "It came from too much smoking and drinking."

We agreed that if he would stop smoking and drinking until after the competition, I would get up at dawn every morning and train with him so that he could have the best chance of winning. What an exhausting job! We hardly rested. Jean's eyes and nose were running all the time; once, he even lost his false teeth in the snow. One afternoon he asked me to describe the sun on the mountains and the shadows on the snow. He told me about the school he had started for blind teenage skiers. We huffed and puffed onward, but we made continual progress.

One day, after intense training, all the blind skiers and their escorts met at the foot of the slalom slope. Jean was to give us a show. He skied full speed down the slope and did not one, but two somersaults. That's when I understood that I was the one who was handicapped, not him. I'd never done anything daring, choosing instead to live a calm, safe life. At that moment I wondered if I had ever really *lived*. As I thought about Jean's goals, I realized that I didn't even know what I wanted from my life.

As it turned out, Jean placed second in the race. He lived two more years. I went home to New England and shared this experience with anyone who would listen. Few did, but I found so much substance in Jean's story that it didn't matter. He had made me realize that those of us who don't dare to live are the truly handicapped in this world.

At home, I sat and made a sketch of the life I wanted. Jean had given me the first tenet: I had to decide exactly what I wanted, so that its validity was absolutely unquestionable. I knew I wanted to do something that would enlighten others and myself. I understood also that I could give more to other people by first developing myself. I wanted to fulfill my potential and be honest with myself, because I knew that I could give my best and attract the best only with total honesty and commitment.

I realized too that I had to take some risks and dare to do what scared me. I wanted to exceed my own limits and experience genuine freedom before I died. Death became an inspiration! If anything was completely certain, it was that I was going to die one day, so my challenge became *living* and giving something of value along the way. It was important to me to view myself as a creative individual. I wanted to fill my life with love, which I believed could best be achieved by accepting myself and accepting others just as we are.

It became clear that I wanted to help people find their own way in life, and help them attain the goals they set for themselves. Since then, it has given me great pleasure to watch people succeed at reaching their goals, and to celebrate triumph after triumph with my clients. Like them, I've faced the things I'm afraid of, continuing despite fearful feelings, which eventually relaxed their hold.

Jean taught me that life is very short, and we mustn't wait too long before mapping out our way. So, what do *you* want to give to yourself and others in the course of this very short time? What are you waiting for?

DARE TO BE TRUE TO YOURSELF

"This above all, to thine own self be true;
And it must follow as the night the day,
Thou canst not then be false to any man."
— William Shakespeare *(Hamlet)*

Our feelings are intelligent, and they give us the information we need to find that place of calm, of knowing what's right for us.

If you're true to yourself, you'll be true to others; if you're not true to yourself, your relationships won't be true either. Outer life happens in parallel with your inner life. If you want to be honest with others, you've got to be honest with yourself first. Do you want the people in your life to be honest? Do you want to be honest and speak the truth from your heart? In the New Testament it is written, "And you shall know the truth and the truth shall set you free." (John 8:32) Truth emerges from our hearts when we're calm, only then do we really know it. Our feelings are intelligent, and they give us the information we need to find that place of calm, of knowing what's right for us. That's living from the inside out.

We learn much that isn't true, and we're taught to ask the world what's right for us. We're encouraged to live from the outside in, a life dictated by the outer world. Not until we look to our hearts to provide us the truth can we know real honesty and become the active leaders of our own lives.

Tapping your emotional intelligence helps you to live authentically by listening to your heart and your head and combining the two. Your truth creates trusting connections with other people, and connects you to your own destiny and to what's meaningful to you.

We are all individuals, and each of us has different goals. What feels right in *your* heart is what's right for you. You're not being self-centered when you ponder the issue of what you want and don't want; it's a simple question of honesty. Being honest with yourself and others is the best foundation for being generous with the world. Allow yourself to think and dream. Most importantly, be honest about what's important to you! And then give life to your dreams!

Some of my most gratifying moments occur when people I'm coaching discover deep in their hearts what's most important to them, what they want to be doing for the rest of their lives. This is why I've urged you so often to write your thoughts on paper. Almost magically, strength and clarity come from articulating your goals, like lifting a veil from your soul and giving it clear directions about where to go.

LEADING YOUR OWN LIFE

Your subconscious can't receive clear instructions if you only "sort of" know what you want. The automatic pilot within you can't guide you forward before you've clearly articulated your goals. Too many people refuse to invest the time necessary to discover what's important to them. If you don't lead yourself, there are plenty of people around who'll try to do the job for you. They'll tell you what you "ought to" and "ought not to" do, according to what they consider important, but no one can take over that position unless you give them the opportunity.

AIM AND MAGIC

In 1953, a new group of students entered Yale University. Three percent of them had clearly defined and expressed goals. Twenty years later, these 3 percent had achieved more of their goals than the 97 percent who hadn't been clear about their objectives. Again, there's a kind of magic in writing down your goals; they take on a more powerful life when they're put on paper, somehow making your dreams more real. Inexplicably, doors begin to open: you connect with just the right person; ideas about how to achieve your goals emerge from unexpected sources. Life takes on new meaning when you can "see" with your inner eye that you're moving closer to your goal. This awareness points you in new directions, opening you to new ways of achieving your aims. A special harmony arises between your inner voice and the world around you.

While you might not always be sure of your direction, you can trust your inner voice to lead you to your destination.

Finding the passion and the faith with which to nourish your dreams assures you a better future. Visualizing it clearly means you're on the right path toward your goal, and your goal is on its path toward you. In contrast, losing sight of your goals is like losing the force that moves you forward in life.

I can't emphasize enough that no matter how you define success, it's a fundamental requirement that your goals come from your heart. Your goal, however, mustn't become an obsession. There's a fine line between being true to your goals and letting them consume you. Often, we do the latter at the expense of success. After you can visualize, articulate, and plan reasonably, you need to learn to relax and let things develop naturally. Finding the passion and the faith with which to nourish your dreams assures you a better future.

THE JOURNEY IS THE REWARD

*"Of course we have our goals in life,
but it's the journey itself that's worth the strife."*
— Karin Boye, Swedish poet

When an old friend asked me how I was doing, I told him I was thoroughly enjoying the journey. "So," he replied, "you've discovered that the journey, not just reaching your goals, holds the true meaning in life?" "Yes," I said, "but the journey wouldn't have been as meaningful if I hadn't had clear goals to guide me."

Learn to enjoy your journey, while remembering that everyday life takes on more meaning when you have goals to lead you. Goals give your journey direction, hope, faith, and a sense of purpose that might otherwise be missing from your life. It's important to remember that you're not simply a product of the goals you achieve. It's the process and the journey you follow in pursuit of your goals—regardless of whether you reach them—that truly defines you.

The Goal Deep in Your Heart
Is a Source of Energy

I encounter many people who lack energy and seem to have lost the ability to enjoy life. Usually, they're in their forties and fifties, though other age groups are certainly not immune. They begin to get tired and lose interest in their endeavors. If this resonates with you, perhaps it's time to reexamine your life.

It's not enough to have goals from long ago that have stayed with you but have lost their attraction, intensity and power to inspire you. Ask yourself what excites you *today*, at this very moment. What makes you happy? What do you hold most dear? What part of your work do you most enjoy? By answering these questions you challenge yourself to plan a life that nurtures the growth of what's most important to you. In order to be successful, you have to engage in activities that resonate with your soul, shedding the "I should's" and embracing the "I want to's."

In addition to practicing the exercises in this book to help develop your emotional intelligence, it's crucial that you uncover goals buried within your inmost self, your heart and soul. When you do, a new energy will emerge, giving you the desire and the strength to create a life full of self-expression. No matter your age, giving life to your core goals will add to your everyday life a richness that's not possible unless you're pursuing what's truly important to you.

You Don't Have to Do Anything!

Many people convince themselves that they "have to" know so much, do so much, and be capable of so much. Seeing life as a series of "have to's" can be destructive. In reality, we don't *have to* do anything. On the contrary, we *choose* to do everything. If, in fact, you were governed by "have to's," you would be renouncing all responsibility for your life. Taking full responsibility for your existence on Earth gives you the key to recognizing your freedom of choice.

Of course, consequences follow from our decisions, and become apparent as we actively make choices. If we decide not to choose, there will be consequences nonetheless. Taking a step back from our lives lets us see that what we are and where we are results from the choices, conscious or not, that we've made along the way. That's why it's so important to try to be mindful of our choices. Take a moment now to give yourself the freedom to choose, and then think about how it would feel to be without it. What are *your* choices?

At the point where emotions interact with thought—where a good mood leads you to think positively—you can expect emotional intelligence to arise. You need to tap this emotional intelligence to make better choices, which create a better life.

Giving yourself the gift of choice can be overwhelming, especially if you're not in the habit. To help yourself, try to remember your happiest moments. Start this journey into the past by searching for five joyful memories. Once you identify them, dig a little deeper and consider why they made you happy. I promise that by doing this exercise you'll uncover new strength and an ability that will illuminate a goal.

Take care, though, not to be swayed by the events in your life that others deem "successful" or "exciting." It's dangerous to let other people's approbation define happiness for you. Instead, focus on those moments in your life that gave you the most pleasure, regardless of others' reactions.

When you've taken time to find out what you really like to do, the next step is to better understand *why* it makes you happy. Knowing will help you develop goals that fit your true nature. Aligning your passions with your goals produces a powerful energy that permeates your entire life. Understanding and giving intention to your goals engenders a depth of meaning that creates a whole that's greater than the sum of its parts. If you feel you've lost the inner fire that propels you along, try to chart a new path for yourself.

Knowing that we have to get up and pay our bills or take

out of the garbage isn't what makes us jump hap- *Never abandon*
pily out of bed every morning. Our goals do that. *a goal that*
Goals have to be rich and attractive enough to *resonates deeply*
hold our attention. Psychologists often say that *in your heart.*
That's the same
we should have realistic goals that are in propor- *as saying "No"*
tion to our abilities. This might be true with respect *to life.*
to some goals, but I encourage you to grant yourself the luxurious pleasure of exciting, ambitious dreams. Dare
to surpass the confining limits that you yourself have set. Let
go of your inhibitions, and reach for a goal that makes your
heart sing and your blood run faster in your veins.

Do you dare to achieve your goal? Do you care what other
people say? Do you care if they laugh, or gloat over the fact
that you didn't succeed? Remember that this isn't about the
rest of the world, it's about *you*. Never abandon a goal that
resonates deeply in your heart. That's the same as saying "No"
to life. Don't give up on anything that really excites you, even
if it looks impossible at first. And don't underestimate the tremendous power that comes from within when you truly believe
in your goal and make a commitment to achieving it. That is
when you can do the "impossible."

THE ROCKING CHAIR TEST

Imagine yourself when you're old, sitting in your rocking chair,
a wool blanket covering your knees. Think of the joy you'll
have remembering all the things you dared to do and say, and
the choices you dared to make because you took control of
your life. Now remember that being true to yourself is the
same as being true to others.

Once, I attended a dinner for Fred, whose firm was honor-
ing him for fifty years' loyal service. As Fred sat facing me, I felt
great respect for his contribution and politely asked, "Have
you been happy these fifty years?" His unhesitating reply was
a shock: "Not for a minute."

I wondered how that could have been possible. "But wasn't there anything you liked about your job during all this time?" I asked. Fred told me that he had spent some time doing carpentry and had really enjoyed it, so I asked why he hadn't pursued that kind of work. He replied that he'd tried once but it hadn't worked out. *Once! Only once! Why not a hundred times?* I thought to myself. But then I reminded myself that these choices weren't mine to make; they were Fred's, and his alone. He had the right to choose as he wished, because his life was his responsibility and no one else's. As I sat staring at his hands, which were obviously made for carpentry, he perceived my disappointment. "Don't be so sad," he said. "I've just bought myself a carpenter's bench."

Think for a moment about all the people in the world who died without ever having chosen to buy themselves their 'carpenter's bench!' When we believe strongly that something is possible, it becomes possible. If we see only impossibility, then that's what we guarantee ourselves. It's been said that perception is one hundred percent of reality. If we believe we're too young, then we *are* too young; if we think we're too weak, we *are* too weak. We need to be consciously aware of how we choose to view the world, because that's the reality in which we put ourselves.

It was a crucial day when I realized that my thoughts control my life. As I said earlier, I had no money when I began my professional journey twenty years ago, but I believed that if I could see my goal clearly enough and wanted it badly enough, I'd be able to achieve it. The hardest part was being honest enough with myself to dare admit out loud what I was lacking. Honesty with ourselves can be difficult if we're out of practice; we need to be completely truthful and admit to what we really want.

Resist that hesitation you feel when you look around and see that no one in your family or your neighborhood has ever done what you want to do. Avoid the trap of believing that you won't succeed just because no one else has. You are unique; no one else can do what you can do the way you can do it. No one else can judge whether your goals are realistic. They can never be in your shoes, and they can never know what you can achieve. It is amazing what you can accomplish when you really want something and are willing to do all it takes to get it.

THREE KINDS OF GOALS

1. The Goal of Acquiring

It's normal to want things. The Western world is flooded with material goods, and wanting to acquire and possess them is a feeling familiar to all of us. We can actually have a lot of fun in the pursuit of getting things that interest us, and subsequently we often develop deep attachments to what we own. Do you remember your attachment to the first thing you saved up for when you were a kid—a bike or a toy?

Some say that the urge to acquire material things has gone too far. I won't moralize about the joys of ownership, but I'll assert that we can't grow as human beings if acquiring is the only thing we strive for. Apart from a roof over your head and enough to eat, *things* are just amusements, not to be confused with necessities. The problem with this kind of amusement is that when we get bored with it, we think we can remedy a lack of meaning in our lives by replacing our old things with new ones. Instead, we create an endless cycle of discontentment. So, while the desire to acquire is an integral and acceptable part of life, it is only one piece of the puzzle.

2. The Goal of Achieving

I'll always remember Nick, a very angry man loaded with ideas that earned him no support from his employer. Nick felt misunderstood and badly treated. He didn't realize how hard it is to receive ideas from a very angry person. After mapping his talents and abilities, and convincing himself that he needn't be different than he was, Nick discovered a new peace. Accepting himself allowed him to look more closely at the anger that had dominated his life.

We needed to get to the root of Nick's anger. A long-time literary critic for a newspaper, he was greatly respected for his knowledge and insight into the world of books. He could talk about literature all day long, but never dared admit to himself that he actually wanted to be an author. When I learned this, I no longer had to wonder why Nick was so angry: he was denying himself the opportunity to achieve a goal that was at the very core of his being.

Once he'd articulated the goal of establishing himself as a writer, it was amazing how strong his commitment became. Now, ten years later, he has published several books. Not all of them have been well received, but that doesn't discourage him from continuing to write with passion. Most importantly, Nick is now engaged in a labor of love, and lives a happier, more fulfilling life because of his achievement. You too can discover the potent magic in uncovering what you really want to achieve.

Thomas came to me feeling dissatisfied with his job as a business manager. He was experiencing a host of conscious and unconscious conflicts around the life choices he had made. For Thomas everything felt like a struggle, and he was tired. Five years away from retirement, he told me that his goal was to endure those five years until he could afford to stop working. In other words, he just wanted to survive.

Through intensive questioning and exploration, we were able to map his talents and abilities. Then came the harder job of discussing his hopes and desires. Finally, Thomas was able to admit that he had long dreamed of living in Spain for six months and learning to speak Spanish. He imagined this time away would also give him the opportunity to work on his inner self and achieve greater peace. Through our work together, he decided to make his dream a reality.

Thomas's wife, who had become frustrated with his pessimistic attitude toward life, was wholly supportive of his decision to go. On the other hand, Thomas dreaded how his employer might react. Before confronting the boss, Thomas put all his thoughts on paper, preparing mentally to present himself and his situation constructively. He succeeded in making his boss understand that he needed a six-month leave of absence in order to achieve a greater understanding in his personal life, which would ultimately benefit his work at the firm. Not only did he receive a positive reaction, but he also became a role model: several of his colleagues have followed suit.

3. The Goal of Being

You can be whoever you want to be, and your awareness of this is fundamental to a fulfilling life. What qualities do you wish to have? I want to be honest. I want to be a loyal friend. I want to be true to myself. I want to be brave. I want to be an expert in my field. I want to be loving, patient, flexible, and open to growth and change. I want to be compassionate and much more. Often I slip and fall, but because I know what qualities I want to have, I can pick myself up again and continue my journey. I believe I can be whatever I want to be, as long as I know precisely what qualities I value. Leading yourself through life's journey is an exciting adventure made up of moments of being. You make choices about who you are and who you want to be at every moment, and by embracing those choices, you can be a person whom you cherish.

We're all looking for closeness and the possibility of contributing our best along the way. Material goods can't fill the vacuum inside us. Meeting our feelings, forgiving, and being true to ourselves will give life the meaning we crave, and the very powerful peace at our deepest core. When we honestly confront ourselves as we are we meet both our best and poorer sides. To meet the one we must also meet and learn to accept the other, and acknowledge that our darker side plays a key role in our contacting a force that's infinite and greater than

Being what you are at this very moment is right, because you are exactly as you should be. By going through the dark of night we walk toward the light of day. The truth will free us to be just as we are.

we are, but is at the same time contained in us. Being what you are at this very moment is *right*, because you are exactly as you should be. By going through the dark of night we walk toward the light of day. The truth will free us to be just as we are.

Ann is a beautiful woman in her fifties. When I first met her I thought, "She's the picture of health." I was amazed to hear her incredible story. For four years Ann had felt trapped in a tough job situation with two employers who couldn't stand each other. Both were her supervisors, and she felt that she was at the mercy of their decisions. She expended so much energy in her frustrating attempts to reconcile these two feuding forces that she neglected her commitment to herself.

Then Ann found out she had cancer. On getting the devastating news, she cried for three days. Somehow, in the midst of her misery, the realization came to her: "If I managed to make myself ill, I can manage to make myself well, too." Regaining her health became her primary goal. As discussed earlier, we've got to believe thoroughly in what we want in order to have any real chance of success. Ann fought bravely to strengthen a belief that might easily not have materialized—the belief that she could get well.

Statistically, the odds were against her. Several doctors told her that her chances were slim, but that didn't erase Ann's hopes for a full recovery. She had to fight not only her illness, but also her doctors' pessimism. Ann's story is both an encouragement to patients who lose hope, and a caution to physicians who discourage the hopes of the sick.

Ann found the Oslo Creativity Center, where cancer patients gather to provide a nurturing environment and a place for healing. There, Ann was able to rid herself of her fear, aggression and hopelessness. She battled her illness because she wanted to live, and her husband and friends supported her and fought right alongside. They all committed themselves to fight for faith and hope, because that's what Ann needed. Somehow, despite the pain and suffering, Ann knew that the "impossible" was possible. In the end, she cured herself.

We've all heard people talk about their tribulations, and it can help us to be mindful of the lessons they learned before we have to experience them for ourselves. As Ann put it, "I'm very grateful for the difficulties I've had. Through them I learned so much about myself and about life. I learned that I have to take care of myself, because no one else bears that responsibility but me. I learned to set limits. I learned to be true to myself, instead of doing what I believed others expected of me. I learned what's important and what's not. I learned that love and closeness are the most essential components of a meaningful life. I learned to distinguish between true and false friends. I learned that life can't be taken for granted. I learned to take care of my body and get enough exercise and rest. I learned that life is lived at this very moment! I learned that there was nothing to wait for; it was life that had been waiting for me."

Heed the call and dare to live!

3

LOVE AND THE REAL MEANING OF LIFE

———◆———

LOVE

However you may define it, love is an endless, life-giving oasis within us. The urge and longing for love is undying. Love is always waiting for us to penetrate the layers that try to smother it. We have the capacity to give and receive love, a luxury we can enjoy all our lives if we choose to.

We can accomplish great things when we feel love in our hearts. Like a laser beam that penetrates where nothing else does, we can accomplish the "impossible" with love guiding us. We can make peace, and we can make our loved ones, our colleagues at work, and even our customers, feel secure. Where there's love, anything is possible, and good things are bound to happen to us and around us.

When we walk around wrapped in a blanket of anguish, fear, and aggression, we emanate negative energy, and will see

Accomplishing something in life isn't simply a matter of what you do, *but also what you* are, *your personality and frame of mind while you're doing.*

only negative results. Our negativity is apparent to the world, whether we intend it to be or not. Under these circumstances, we're often better off staying at home in bed, wrapped up in our blanket. We can then protect not only ourselves, but also those who feel the effects of our negativity, directly or indirectly. Try going out and selling when you're in one of these states—it just doesn't work.

Accomplishing something in life isn't simply a matter of what you *do*, but also what you *are*, your personality and frame of mind while you're doing. When you're loving and peaceful inside, you make space for others to "be." You might also want to reexamine your continual need to be "accomplishing." Perhaps we can serve as catalysts and bring out the best in those around us. There's something about us that can't always be defined, something positive but invisible that emanates from us. This "something" can create a loving atmosphere, conducive to making things happen that ordinarily don't.

In such an atmosphere miracles do happen. This power was true when Gandhi succeeded in liberating India from British rule. No force was used; no war was started. He led a nonviolent movement that won greater victories than many wars do. When we're filled with love we have power and strength. If we're not in contact with the love inside us, we may feel powerless.

Putting love first implies trying to create a better world. From the moment we choose to cleanse ourselves of negativity and focus on love instead, the rest of our life will fall into place. This certainly doesn't mean that our lives won't have their share of hardships and pain, but love in its truest sense is more powerful than suffering. Making room for love is a continual process, requiring us to confront and fight our negativity repeatedly in order to rediscover our love. A participant at one of my seminars compared it to "cleaning out the barn every day."

To Be Loved Just as I am

Once, in a convent, I met a wonderful human being. Sister Irene spoke so gently that it was easy to open my weary heart to her, the first time as a mature woman that I opened myself completely. I laid bare my sorrow and desperation. Regardless of what I told her, Sister Irene remained serene. She had a loving presence that made me feel confident that I would get through my divorce crisis. It felt as though I were being given a great gift. She let me be myself with her and never corrected or judged me.

In the confines of my tiny, sparse cloister cell, I cried for joy because so much love had been given to me. In the shower that night I let the warm water run down my back, and the more I relaxed, the more I realized how much love I had missed out on because I hadn't been receptive to it. I let the water symbolize all the love that had previously been given to me that I had been unable to accept. It felt miraculous to open to all that love!

When I saw Sister Irene at the evening meal, I wanted to pick her up and dance her around the room in gratitude for all the love she had given me. (I refrained.) Several days later, when we said farewell, she looked so tiny, so light and loving in her cowl and nun's robe that I couldn't contain myself. I picked her up and whirled her around until she shouted with joy.

Sister Irene was seventy years old. I have much to thank her for. She made me realize that we are all good enough, despite what we've done in the past, and most importantly, that we all deserve to be loved.

What is love? The question has been studied from so many angles that there are as many answers as there are people. With

Sister Irene it was unconditional acceptance, which is how I experience love.

Love or Control

Often we confuse love with control. Many children interpret what their parents say as meaning: "I love you if you do well in school, if you behave and do what I say; if not, I can't love you as much." Many of us grow up feeling that we have to earn love by fulfilling expectations and obligations. That's not love; that's control. Instead, emotionally intelligent parents might say: "You are my child and I'll always love you, whatever you do. I might not always like what you do, but I love you."

Love or Duty

Sometimes it's hard to tell the difference between doing and giving. Many participants in my seminars have aging parents, and feel obliged to care for them, which is a source of strain and frustration for some. Their parents want them to visit more often, whether at home or in the hospital, and may have all sorts of expectations. The children feel inadequate, guilt-ridden and powerless, and often become angry. This notion of duty wears on both the parents and the children.

Kate, whose mother was in a retirement home, was worn out and despairing. At the first seminar, she found it depressing to hear that she was responsible for her own life—the responsibility felt overwhelming to her. Later, when Kate realized that she had the right to make choices that felt right to her, she grew to accept it. The idea of being responsible for her own life gave her the freedom to be true to herself, which implies being true to others as well. Kate developed the courage to feel which choices she wanted to live with, choices that made her happier and thereby better able to make her mother happy.

Most people also confuse doing with giving. If Kate felt fatigued and angry every time she visited, what, then, was she really giving to her mother? A face to look at, perhaps, but Kate was simultaneously signaling her weariness and anger to the very person she was trying to help. Love is contagious, as are many other feelings.

WE CHOOSE TO DO EVERYTHING

In the seminar, we focused on the choices Kate faced. In order to give her freedom to choose, we performed a rather provocative exercise. Try the following:

Say to yourself: "I don't *have to* do anything. There isn't one thing in the world that I *have to* do." It might sound ridiculous at first, but play with the idea for a while. Perhaps there are things that you feel you have to do, but try to resist believing that you're duty-bound to do anything. Examine the validity of those obligations.

You might say, "I have to eat." No, history is filled with martyrs who starved themselves to death. "But I have to go to work." No, you just *think* you have to. A great many people don't go to work, and you could choose to be like them. You really don't *have to* do anything. Well, there's one exception. We all *have to* die; no one gets out of here alive.

We don't *have to* anything. We *choose* everything, and our choices have consequences. We're free, and we don't *have to* anything because we're responsible for our own lives. Remember that if others were responsible for us, we really would *have to*, but as we alone are responsible for ourselves, we're free to choose every second of the day—a truth we need to remember always.

After completing this exercise, we continued asking Kate probing questions about what she really wanted. She wanted to visit her mother, but she didn't want to *have to* do it so often. Now she was tapping her emotional intelligence and

Taking responsibility for your life translates into having something to give. making the choice that felt right to her. Through some soul searching, Kate decided that twice a week felt reasonable to her. She had reasoned using her emotions, checking both her head and heart for the solution to her dilemma. She realized that during two weekly visits she would have much more to give to her mother than she'd had when anger and resentment were consuming her. She was happy to see her mother, and her mother would feel that joy.

Taking responsibility for your life translates into having something to give. When you take care of yourself first, you are much better able to take care of others. There are crisis situations when you'll need to give more than you usually want to. It's important to be there for a friend in need even though your report is due on Monday. We need to search our hearts for how to choose and prioritize. Taking responsibility for our lives means different choices to different people. Always choose what's right for you.

OUR LOVING SELF

Everyone yearns for love. After life's basic necessities, we want love more than anything else in the world. Why then, you might ask, is love not first on our list of priorities? If love is so central to our existence, how can we lose sight of it? We have an endless, though perhaps undiscovered and unreleased, capacity for love. It's in the child that still lives deep inside each of us. Our challenge is to get in touch with this love, and we can't do that until we can remove the obstacles that block our access to it.

Many people who have attended my seminars say that they long for peace of mind above all. I try to impress upon them that we can only achieve peace of mind if we make love our top priority. Paranoia, confusion and madness result from not letting go of our fear and anger. We achieve peace of mind when we choose love instead of hanging on to negative emotions. The love within us doesn't die, but it can seem to disappear behind the pain. Layers of fear and anger cover our love and paralyze us, changing us into antagonistic individuals. Unless we're in touch with the love inside us, our actions can become irrational and very unwise.

There can be no wisdom without love—yet another reason why it's so important to make a primary goal of integrating our negative emotions by feeling them fully, so that we can find the way back to love. Love is peace; to abandon love is pain.

Our greatest enemy isn't in the world around us; it lives inside us. We need to stop being so angry with ourselves! Once, my negativity was so great that I thought I was going to beat myself to death. Since then I've chosen to treat myself with love and kindness, but it took time to learn how. Treating myself badly never made me feel better, only worse. After tearing myself down, I had less to give to other people. Now my goal each day is to love, and things just seem to fall into place.

Love in its truest form is unconditional. You deserve to be loved now and forever, just as you are this minute. As we move through life, we discover that we get love only when we give it. Often, we receive love without being aware of it. Think how blessed we would feel if we could connect with people in a way that makes us aware of their love and ours! Consider what we're missing when we're unaware.

Awareness of love removes the veil of negativity with which we so often cover ourselves. Negative feelings aren't wrong; they just exist. Knowing that puts us in a position to get free if we integrate them by feeling them. Passive, nonintegrated feelings cover up the wisdom within us. We need to remove the veil to see clearly and live more positively. Without impediment, love becomes an intuitive relationship with one's own inner voice. This healthy relationship leads to positive, gratifying feelings: acceptance, compassion, kindness, generosity, open-mindedness and peace of mind.

Disregarding our inner voice leads to painful loss of love and loss of direction at the same time. Our inner wisdom is intimately tied to our ability to love ourselves and those around us. It's vital to learn to trust our inner self to guide us to a more loving life. When we learn to focus on the love within us, we embark on a fabulous journey from pain to inner peace. Unfortunately, most of us must experience considerable pain before we can begin the trip.

To feel your emotions fully can be painful, but every time you dare to feel fully, you move forward. The great success that the leaders that I coach achieve invariably comes from 'burning away' the feelings that have been stopping them. These people don't have emotional problems and they're not sick— they just acknowledge that there's no gain without pain, and the reward for feeling the pain fully is enormous. Feeling painful emotions is a hard sell: we don't want pain, we want joy and peace and love, but they don't come without feeling and integrating all your negative feelings.

There are multiple layers of gray clouds for all of us. When we go through them by feeling fully and understanding the information our feelings give us, we find blue skies. When new gray clouds appear, we repeat the exercise, having learned that the reward is more peaceful sunshine, clearer thinking and direction, and sure contact with the inner voice, our own leader who guides us.

Because all our thoughts directly affect the world around us, we can easily understand that our negative thoughts create negative results. Similarly, positive, loving thoughts generate positive effects. It's comforting to know that we have the power to choose whether to sow positive or negative seeds. Dandelions grow quickly; it's important to weed them out by choosing love and positive thinking as our most important goal.

There's nothing inherently wrong with weeds, but they can strangle more nourishing plants that could grow strong and healthy in their absence. We can't be lazy and ignore the occasional dandelions that crop up; they can grow so big and strong that there's no space left for our rose bushes. My "garden" was once in this condition, but through hard work I created room for life's more precious flowers. I just need to remember to weed periodically. I get rid of my mental dandelions by writing them out of me, feeling them at the same time. In this manner, I clear space for the most beautiful plants— love and positive thoughts.

LOVE—THE GREATEST RESPONSIBILITY OF ALL

Part of taking responsibility for your life includes getting in touch with all the love and positive thoughts within you, which is another way of taking care of others. Think of how your love and inner peace gently touches the people who share your life. If everyone were willing and able to take such responsibility, discord, hatred and war might become things of the past.

I have a childish dream, but one that's important to me and compels me to action every day. I'll share it, and maybe it can become your dream, too. The dream is best illustrated by a story titled "The Hundredth Monkey." Troops of monkeys lived on an isolated island. One day, one of them decided to wash his potato so that he wouldn't have to eat the earth that was stuck to it. Soon, many other monkeys began washing their potatoes too. Amazingly, by the time the hundredth monkey had followed suit, all the monkeys on the island began washing their potatoes!

Perhaps you and I could really do something for this world if we were willing to "wash our potatoes" and inspire others to do the same. Imagine all humanity acting in this manner! It's important to hope and dream.

Conversing with a philosophy teacher, I said, "Throughout history, philosophers have changed how they regard life. Is there one thing that you can say is certain and won't change?"

"The only thing we really know," he replied, "is that we must go on hoping."

I want to share with you the hope that supports me in life. I believe we can create a loving world, safe for all, if we choose love as our primary goal.

THE MEANING OF LIFE

Throughout the ages people have asked what is the meaning of life: "Who am I? Why am I here on Earth?" In search of answers to these eternal questions, all of us — the nuclear physicist and the child, the homeless person and the millionaire, the priest and the housewife, the Christian and the Muslim — are on equal footing. We're all entitled to ask these questions, but none of us can really know the "right" answer for anyone else.

It's possible that life has no inherent universal meaning. It appears to me that we have to give life a meaning through our thoughts and actions, a meaning in harmony with our own inner voice. It is *within* ourselves that we find the secret of life, the meaning that so many seek.

When we create some degree of meaning in life, all our endeavors begin to take on meaning. My mission in life is to bring out the hidden resources in others and in myself in order to be able to create the life we want. It gives me great joy, and it feels right to me, and that's sufficient—*I'm following my inner voice.* Others believe differently, but I believe everyone has a mission in life, and when they discover what it is, their lives will become easier, richer and more meaningful. In my coaching I see this happening again and again.

During my travels, I habitually ask the same question of cab drivers: "Do you like your work?" If the answer is anything less than a definite yes, that driver clearly hasn't yet found his mission in life. If the answer is yes, I push forward. "What do you like about your job?" It's interesting how varied the responses are from the ones who really love their jobs.

A cabby in Florida preferred to drive at night, because he wanted to be available when people really needed him. He was well aware of the fact that he was a "social worker" in the invisible social system of the street, and he loved his position. What mattered to him was being able to help people who felt alone, lost or depressed. He felt he had the world's best job, but that very few people understood this. It was enough for him that *he* understood it. This man had found the meaning in his life.

A cab driver in Norway liked to help elderly people, because they often seemed lonesome and had no one else to talk to. He loved his job. A third driver, who wasn't the talkative type, apparently found great pleasure in his job. He was the practical type and could handle almost anything—baby carriage, wheelchair, seven suitcases and a bunch of flowers—no problem, this was his way of giving, and it obviously made him very happy. Then there was the cabby who preferred driving a minivan so he could entertain a bigger audience with stories and songs.

We're all motivated by different things, but we can all give meaning to our undertakings. What makes you happy? If you know the answer, you've already found the key to giving your life meaning.

At a seminar, Amy began to discover the meaning of her existence. There were times when she didn't want to live anymore, but over time she came to feel that her experiences had given her insight into the human condition. Developing a greater understanding of life made her want to share her perceptions with others. Amy is now a teacher and has begun writing children's stories about the human heart. She came to realize that her mission was to share her ideas about life through the written word.

What's *your* mission? Whether you're aware of it or not, you know the answer deep inside yourself. Ask yourself again

What's meaningful to you? What makes you happy? What makes your heart rejoice? and again, until you find what's truly important to you. It can take time, so be patient. What's meaningful to you? What makes you happy? What makes your heart rejoice?

We humans are delicate creatures, and we're confronted with many obstacles that prevent us from doing what really makes us happy and gives our lives meaning. It makes Amy happy to write, but something still keeps her from enjoying it fully. She has a "doomsday" feeling and believes that she'll be punished if she gets *too* happy. She's afraid that she'll lose her loved ones if she succumbs to excessive pride, and while she knows that her fear is irrational, it's there with her. Amy has decided to see a psychologist, with whom she's working through her fear. Amy's anxiety stands between her and her full development. By confronting her feelings, she's coming closer to achieving her goal of writing freely and without fear.

ONLY YOU CAN GIVE YOUR LIFE MEANING

It feels good to know that we're needed. Feeling needed gives life meaning. In times of widespread unemployment, many people find that their services and talents are not in demand. Life may seem meaningless without work. At such times, it's vital to remember that you, and only you, can give your life significance. Regardless of your present circumstances you still have a purpose in the world. (You might disagree, but I am one hundred percent certain that you wouldn't be in this world unless there was some reason for your being here.)

"The point is to find the work that needs to be done." These words, spoken by Magda, a woman who has been fishing in Norway for the past thirty years, appeared in an interview in one of Norway's leading newspapers. Magda's life is full of hard work, tough conditions and great love. When she and her husband, Peter, first met, it was "as if we were cemented together for all time." Peter still refers to his wife as "a miracle of a woman." They plunged headlong into life together, raised a family, and worked hard when the sea raged and when it was quiet. Both say that life has been an amusing and an exhausting adventure. Neither speaks grandly of the "meaning of life," but when we read about them, we under-

Without exception, all who give meaning to their own lives give to the rest of the world.

stand that Magda and Peter see meaning in working for themselves and for society, and in doing their work with love. They believe that life needs them, and the key lies in what Magda says about seeing what needs to be done around her.

Many people lack self-confidence and feel that they have nothing to give to others. In this regard, the story of Arne holds a lesson for us all. Arne has written a remarkable book, *This is My Life.* His autobiography is unusual in that Arne suffers from Down's syndrome. He feels, nonetheless, that his life has been so rich and exciting that he wants to share it with others. Arne has worked in a canteen, in a church, as a postman and as an actor. No one crosses his path without an embrace. "I am a happy man," he says.

To read about Arne is to learn about a life full of meaning. He makes himself happy, he makes those around him happy, and he has been a role model who gives new ideas and meaning to everyone he meets. With his congenital handicap Arne could easily have been marginalized, but he has proven to the world that he has more to give than meets the eye. Without exception, all who give meaning to their own lives give to the rest of the world.

We're accustomed to estimating our own and other people's worth on the basis of what we do and the financial rewards we derive. However, we give as much by just *being* as by doing. Perhaps you feel that your reason for being is to give love. If so, you bring this reason for just *being* with you everywhere: into the elevator, onto the street, to the grocery store, to other countries, everywhere you go.

To live fully is to enjoy life right now, to be in the moment.

Because this moment is all we have for certain, it's most important to create meaning right now. As you read this, another moment has already passed. We wait for epiphanies, but in reality, this instant is all that we are guaranteed. Of people from the West, a man from India said, "When you people sit, you're waiting to stand up. When you stand, you're waiting to walk. But when we in India sit, we sit. When we walk, we walk. And when we lie down, we lie down."

As children, we couldn't wait to start grade school. There, we looked forward to finishing so we could start college, then to getting married and having children, then to the time when our children had grown up, then to retirement. *Then* life would really begin! Clearly, it's foolish to postpone enjoying life just because you assume (usually erroneously) that everything will be so much better later. "Remember to live while you are alive, remember to love when you dare to, " says Piet Hein.

The only time we possess for certain is this moment. My mother often told me that it was important to value the uniqueness of the moment, bind it to my heart and "put a gold frame around it." It is a good exercise to train the eye and the heart to see that this very second is such a precious moment.

I used to travel on vacation with Roberta and her husband, Ben. He was eager to explore the new places we visited. Roberta, however, dreamed of the East Coast when we were on the West Coast; she missed the sun when it was raining, and the rain when it was sunny! Her basic attitude seemed to be: "If only things were different, I would be happy." I learned a great deal from her.

Things are the way they are. The art of living requires us to accept the facts of life and make the best of them. Treasure is staring us right in the face at this very moment if we choose to see it. To live fully is to enjoy life right now, to be in the moment. There's no reason to put off living. There is deep wisdom and regret in the words "All those days that came and went, I didn't realize that they were life itself."

Life is a great mystery, and we stumble onward together. The mystery renders life exciting and gives it meaning. We learn along the way, from ourselves and from others. Hopefully, we'll never learn all there is to know about life and about being human, because then the pleasure of life would be gone; the journey would be over.

We go through life, each in his or her own way, with different hopes, expectations, experiences and treasures to give to each other. There's much to celebrate on the way, if we choose to do so. Let's try to celebrate much more, and feel that life has meaning because we choose to live in the present, at this very moment. Let's celebrate today!

4

Learning to Soar:

Exercises in Managing

Your Feelings

—◆—

The recurrent theme of this book is that to influence your life in an effective way you need to tap the power of your emotional intelligence. All personal growth depends on acknowledging and facing one's feelings. By doing so, we can build a solid foundation from which we can manage ourselves and lead our lives to success and meaning. This chapter will give you an overall view of the effective exercises that have proven in many seminars to be helpful to a wide range of participants facing all sorts of difficulties.

We are all at different emotional stages in life. For some of us life is calm, with a little ripple on the water now and then. For others there's a full storm and mountainous waves. Most of us live an emotional life somewhere between the extremes. This book was written for all of us. Find the exercises that work best for you. As you begin managing your most challenging emotions, it's very easy to tap into the power of your emotional intelligence.

1. THE CHECK-IN EXERCISE

Get in touch with your feelings

Try to use this exercise several times a day to make sure you're in touch with our feelings. If you don't know what you're feeling and you don't check in on your feelings, you can't tap your emotional intelligence. Feeling little is a sign of trouble: you might, for example, be cut off from your feelings by running too fast or being too ambitious. This can blind you to the signals you're sending out. It can keep you from making wise decisions by asking your head and your heart. It can prevent you from connecting with people and influencing them the way you want to, because you've lost the only tool to guide you: your feelings. You might think you're doing brilliantly, but watch the results for the real story of what's going on inside you. Your feelings will be communicated to people, but you won't have a clue about what those emotions are saying. The leaders I coach take this tool very seriously every day.

* *Sense: What are you feeling? Do you sense that your body is trying to tell you something? Is your body tense, anxious, relaxed? Where in your body do you sense this—in your heart, in your stomach?*

* *Identify the feeling: Whatever you're feeling, feel the feeling—are you angry, afraid, relieved?*

* *Identify and access the feeling behind the initial feeling: What feelings are hiding behind the first feelings? Feel*

those feelings! Are you hurting? Do you feel joy? Do you feel lonely?

❧ *Information: What is the feeling telling you?*

❧ *Information: What does your intellect tell you is a good action to take?*

❧ *Double-check: Does it feel right, or might there be an even better way?*

❧ *Action: Don't give in until your heart and head are aligned.*

2. The Writing Exercise

Write out your feelings

When you have an overflow of emotions, this is an excellent tool. Writing out your feelings is a means of integrating yourself and getting relief by emptying yourself; reducing the strain that negative emotions place on you. It's also a great way to learn about yourself, because you can often see and understand better from the "outside" when you read what you've written. Here are some guidelines that might be helpful in your writing:

❧ *You can write whenever and wherever you want.*

❧ *Write down exactly what you think and feel.*

❧ *Don't censor anything. Write everything you think but don't dare say aloud. Don't be cautious in your writing.*

❧ *Write in a way that feels like it's clearing out all your feelings.*

❧ *Read what you've written. This will increase your awareness of your true emotions and teach you to know what your feelings are telling you.*

❀ *Become aware of your blind spots. Is anything you're writing surprising you? That's where your blind spots are, and that's where you need to learn to see.*

❀ *Take what you've written and put it away, or tear it in pieces and throw it away.*

❀ *Don't send letters you've written in anger: If you write thirty such letters, perhaps the last one might be appropriate to mail.*

❀ *Read your writing again and again to check that you've done your best to release all your negative emotions. Remember that this restores your power over yourself.*

The more we write, the more we reduce the strain on our minds, bodies and souls. When that strain has been channeled away, we can see our lives more clearly. Sometimes, we need to literally "see our feelings" written on paper to make sense of them. When we do, our emotions no longer surprise and confuse us, and we can break the vicious cycle of negative feelings breeding negative results. The outcome is a calm at your center that translates into a powerful sense of freedom and possibility.

Your feelings are smart, they never lie, and they carry important information about you and your life. Let yourself be angry more often, and write it out each time. It's important that you write *to get rid of* your anger. The effect of writing to get rid of anger is freedom and power. (If you write out your feelings with the goal of replaying them, holding on to them instead of wanting to be rid of them, you'll sink deeper into trouble.)

To be able to tap all of your emotional intelligence, do these exercises. You are now in charge of your own life, you're stronger, maybe you feel that you are on top of the table instead of under it (for a while, at least—it's important to do the writing exercise again and again every time you feel that your feelings are overflowing).

3. The Tape Recorder Exercise

Express your thoughts and feelings on tape

If you'd rather not write, or want an additional option, you can talk out your feelings onto tape. Like writing, taping allows you to say whatever you like, and your verbalized thoughts and emotions can't hurt anyone.

❂ *Find a place where you feel sure no one can hear you.*

❂ *If you need to direct your negative emotions to a person, start by visualizing that individual in front of you as you speak into the microphone.*

❂ *Don't cut your speaking short. Push yourself to articulate all your thoughts and feelings.*

❂ *Talk, shout, scream—don't hold anything back.*

When you're finished, listen to the tape as often as you need to. The repetition will help you clarify what you're really feeling and the physical sensations you're experiencing. Jack, a manager I coached, was facing some tough problems at work and chose to try this method. He managed to put his feelings into spoken words and was able to integrate and cleanse himself of a lot of anger and aggression. "You know," he said to me, "I didn't have the courage to listen to the tape until several days later." I knew from firsthand experience what he was talking about. Whatever exercises you use to work through your emotions, it is important that you remember to take your time and move at your own pace.

4. The Hitting Exercise

Punch until you hit your feelings!

Repressed emotions affect both mind and body. They manifest in our bodies in the form of tension, headaches, aching muscles, and other forms of pain and discomfort. Because of the close mind/body connection, letting yourself hit an object with uninhibited aggression can help you get in contact with your feelings.

For some people, especially for women, this exercise might be difficult at first. Unlike men, women are taught as children not to resort to physical aggression. The only rule in this exercise is that you hit inanimate objects, not people or animals!

❀ *Find a place where you can scream if you want.*

❀ *Find something you can hit that won't cause you harm. A mattress might work, or you could roll up a newspaper and hit the wall or a table with it.*

❀ *Hit until you can't hit any more.*

❀ *Scream with no restraint whatsoever.*

In the process, or perhaps immediately after, tears are likely to flow. Allow yourself to experience whatever emotions emerge. Also, let yourself say or scream whatever thoughts or feelings enter your head or heart. Then, as described above, take the time to write out or speak into a tape recorder whatever you're experiencing. Getting out your aggression physically isn't sufficient by itself to integrate your emotions and cleanse yourself of those difficult ones.

Your car is an excellent place to scream. It can be fun to pretend you're talking on the car phone. You can also hit the seat, or pull over and write, till you find some peace. (A good friend of mine discovered that amusement parks are a good alternative: who'll notice if you scream on a roller coaster?) Pounding on something has helped many people reach their repressed emotions. To achieve real results it's best to follow up with exercises that are more quieting.

5. The 'Dip' Exercise

Confronting your feelings

This is a good way to integrate your feelings and get closer to yourself, but it takes some repetition and practice. Start with pen and paper or a tape recorder. The advantage of this technique is that you can eventually practice it wherever and whenever you choose.

❀ *Be aware that you're fighting. You simply will not feel.*

❀ *Breathe deeply for a few minutes. Stay aware of your breathing, aware of each inhalation and exhalation. This is a way of being in control of yourself.*

❀ *Imagine that you're experiencing the feelings coming and going.*

❀ *'Dip' into your emotions, confront them and get totally immersed in them.*

❀ *Stay in your feelings, acknowledge them, and feel them until they let go of you. It's like dipping into cold water: after a while it doesn't feel as bad. Get out when you can't stand it anymore.*

When you can make room for your pain, and are on the cusp of pain with your full consciousness, then you can find your own vantage point. When you've experienced the whole feeling, it will fade.

If we truly want to develop as people, we can't avoid our

feelings. We have to move *through* them instead. We pressure ourselves constantly to know and understand "things," but understanding in our heads can't move us forward without feeling and understanding our emotions. Self-understanding is a prerequisite for all other knowledge. Even if we do enough, or know enough, we must also *feel* enough.

As an example, let's look at a difficult situation that's familiar to many of us. Imagine that the relationship between you and your lover has ended. You might be relieved at first, and surprised that the break wasn't as painful as you had feared. You're optimistic: everything will be fine. Later you begin to grieve. The separation is hard, but you're unwilling to acknowledge how hard it really is. At that critical moment, when you're just about to divorce yourself from the feelings and repress them, you decide instead to confront your feelings.

You become aware of your breathing for a few minutes, and then you dip into your feelings in order to put your grief behind you. The pain distresses you, but the process feels right. You're able to welcome these feelings and liberate them. It's only through that integration of emotions that we feel liberated. We're no longer in a battle of conflicting emotions. Instead we have greater clarity. We can feel the pain without becoming involved in its drama. We have more freedom of movement, because we dip in or step out of our feelings at will. We speed up our own development this way.

Sooner or later, we all experience the loss of a loved one. One of my closest friends died of cancer. I was overcome with grief but somehow found the strength to welcome my feelings about her death. She and I were very close, and I missed her dearly. I sat for hours and relived the many happy times we shared. In my mind and heart she was present, real and wise. I cried and cried, and grieved over my loss. After some time, my feelings changed from grief to profound gratitude for the rich experiences we had had together, and for the fact that I had been able to know such a wonderful person.

My friend will live inside me for the rest of my life, and I want to keep it that way. At the same time, I needed to move through my grief so that it could no longer consume me. We have to practice these exercises over and over to really work through our emotions.

Many people believe that holding on to their grief about loved ones is a way of paying homage to the deceased. I couldn't disagree more. When we perpetuate our grief, it consumes us in a way that precludes our having anything to give to those around us who remain alive and well. We need to give ourselves time to experience our grief, and by doing so we can let go of it. If we don't confront our feelings of grief and move through them properly, subsequent heartaches become that much harder to bear; our next grief will add to the old.

Life isn't always easy, but no one ever said it was supposed to be. We need courage to confront our feelings, but even greater freedom and joy awaits us when we can. If you're not in the habit of welcoming unpleasant emotions, I recommend doing Exercise 1 or 2 first, and then move on to 3 if that feels right to you. Later on, when you feel ready, you can try Exercise 4.

6. THE CREATIVE EXERCISE

Express yourself through art

When you're feeling emotions that are difficult to express through the other exercises, let your creativity take over; you can draw, paint or sculpt what you feel. But "art" isn't limited to these forms. You can express your emotions through music, dance, cooking or gardening.

My friend Tracy would unleash her anger and frustrations by furiously digging a new area in her garden. She'd "express" contentment by planting new flowers and shrubs, and uneasiness by moving them around the garden. She'd express grief and sorrow for departed loved ones by planting the flowers that were their favorites. Tracy's garden has grown and changed, and through it all it was uniquely hers. It has given other people great joy and peacefulness, and has given Tracy a wonderful way to express herself.

Expression through art can be therapeutic; you can really feel the emotion, let it become part of you, create something while you feel it, and when you've released the emotion you have something to show for it.

Paul's mother told me, "I remember when Paul was fifteen. Quite suddenly, he became very unhappy and experienced his first emotional crisis. He was so confused and sad that I resolved to let him stay home from school for a while. The only thing that interested him was drawing. I went and bought new colors and decided to draw and paint with him. Paul didn't touch the lovely colors I'd bought; he wanted only the black and brown. After a few days, the colors he chose were lighter and brighter."

Art was Paul's way of experiencing his feelings and moving through them. It's a great exercise, which gets you in touch with your subconscious and allows you to confront the feelings buried there. Enjoy doing your art: it does you a world of good and therefore it benefits others too.

7. THE SHARING EXERCISE

To share is to live

Paul discovered the secret of sharing. He kept his thoughts and feelings to himself for many years, but one day he couldn't keep it all inside anymore. His heart had been broken, and it was too much for him to bear alone. He knew he had to confide in someone, otherwise life felt too difficult. He decided to go to his colleague, Peter, with whom he had a good relationship.

To Paul's surprise, Peter shared a similar experience. After some discussion, it was clear to Paul that the opportunity to tell his story made him feel better. Sharing his feelings with someone who was willing to take the time to listen and talk about himself was rich and helpful. Sharing and compassion are really at the core of the human experience. To share is to live.

It takes a lot of courage, but sharing has a magical effect on everyone involved. Still, it can be a delicate matter. Some people believe they're sharing when they're actually "throwing up" on each other. We need to be aware of the difference, which is why it's wise, before you engage in sharing, to remove the most intensely charged feelings by practicing the exercises that suit you. What you share is just as legitimate without threatening the one you need to share it with.

Most of us can listen to the aching of a broken heart without being overly affected. It's more difficult to cope with listening to someone accuse us of having wronged them while they are still full of anger toward us. This is simply too demanding for most individuals. If, nevertheless, you choose to "throw up," it's wise to divide your wrath among several people, not give it only to your loved ones.

A director once said to me, "Something slams shut inside me when someone speaks to me in anger." Thus, it's best to go through your most negative feelings alone before sharing them with others. Remember that what you send out into the world is what you get back.

8. MENTAL TRAINING

Peaceful time

Giving yourself fifteen or twenty minutes of quiet before your day begins, before a meeting or a difficult conversation, is the best investment you can make. If you're experiencing a lot of difficulty, practice the writing or tape exercise first, or even the dip exercise. Use the one that's most effective for you. After any of these, you can move on to mental training.

There are many methods of mental training. Many years' experience has shown me one that helps people see more clearly. Specifically, it helps you see when you're on the verge of walking into a pitfall. Using it, you're likely to find that solutions to your problems and challenges arise quickly from the wise place within you.

Mental training brings out both the leader and the coach in you, and cuts through obsolete habits and negative thoughts. The exercises make you see your problems more objectively by leading you to a meditative place inside you, where you know what's best to do. After having practiced mental training for a while, you'll reach a place where you can fully trust the direction revealed to you. Getting in touch with your inner voice this way makes it easier to hear as it advises you how to live.

At ninety-one years of age, Elsa worked to get in touch with her inner voice by seeking quiet every day. "If I had listened to my inner voice when I was young, I could have done so much more during my lifetime." Her clarity and peace of mind made quite an impression.

Notice all of the thoughts that whirl around in your head. Stop and listen to them. It's impossible to achieve full clarity amidst so much thought. You need to cut out stream-of-conscious thinking to become objective about your problems.

There are many techniques for training your mind. This one can yield positive results:

❊ *Set aside twenty minutes for yourself.*

❊ *Sit quietly alone with your eyes closed.*

❊ *Breathe deeply.*

❊ *Try not to think of anything in particular.*

If you fall back into your usual way of thinking, try again until your thoughts get quieter and you feel peaceful. It usually takes some time to master this technique. To help quiet your thoughts you can try concentrating on your fingers:

❋ *Sit on a chair without arms.*

❋ *Close your eyes.*

❋ *Breathe deeply for a while.*

❋ *Let your right hand hang loosely.*

❋ *Concentrate on your right hand.*

❋ *Gently focus on one finger at a time, again and again.*

When I suggest that you be gentle, it's because you needn't force yourself to concentrate. Focus lightly on one finger at a time for fifteen or twenty minutes. Be easy on yourself if you find it hard to concentrate fully on your hand; if your thoughts begin to wander just gently guide them back to your thumb, index finger, middle finger, fourth finger, fifth finger, and back to your thumb again. As you continue this way, you'll begin to feel how quiet you become after a short while.

Eventually, you can develop your own system as your inner voice helps you figure out what you need. Whatever way you choose, it's important to practice being quiet inside every day. Even the bathroom can become your oasis if you have no other options! There's security in quietude, even under the most difficult circumstances.

In the process of developing themselves, most people *read* book after book. This book won't help you unless you practice the exercises. They'll get you in touch with your inner voice. In it lies your emotional intelligence and the art of leading yourself. It tells you the right choices to make. Only your quiet inner voice can tell you what you need to know.

There are lots of ways to find quietude and contact your inner voice. I can offer you a menu that has worked for others, but only you can choose to do these exercises; no one else can do the work for you.

Many of us avoid quiet, because getting to know ourselves isn't always pleasant. But we need to see ourselves clearly in order to *lead* our lives. If we refuse to become aware of our feelings and our choices, the passion of our lives disappears, and we become unconscious, dull human beings.

Remember that you're continually making choices. You make them all day—you chose to get up this morning, or maybe you chose to stay in bed. Even not choosing is a choice. Consciously or unconsciously, you choose every second of the day.

You are what you are and where you are as a result of the choices you've made up to the present moment. If you believe that what happens to you has less to do with the choices you make than with external influences, you have no chance of influencing your life positively. Regardless of what happens, you can choose how you'll relate to the situations you're faced with. It's not always what happens that's so important, but the choices you make in response to what happens.

You are unique. No one has ever been or will be like you. It's crucial that you find out what your unique person really wants. Only you have responsibility for your life. And because you have the right and the potential to choose, you are free.

5

Getting Unblocked

—◆—

Stories about Grownups

These stories illustrate how we can influence and manage a variety of situations.

An Accident before
an Important Meeting

Harry, a businessman on his way to one of the most important meetings of his career, scraped the entire left side of his brand-new car on a cement post in the parking lot. He was shattered that he could have been so careless. When Harry reached his meeting, he couldn't concentrate. He was preoccupied with the accident: the repairs were going to be expensive, and he felt terrible.

Though his thoughts were in turmoil, Harry remembered that he had learned to work through his feelings on paper. Right there in the meeting, he put his pen to paper: "How could you be such an idiot! A cement post. Damn it, won't you ever learn to pay attention? It really hurts to have had an accident. It's so dumb to wreck a brand-new car." Harry continued to write down his every thought. He had to get them out until they were no longer consuming him. Eventually he reached the conclusion that he had the right to make a mistake, that it was only human. After all, a car is just a car. The important thing was that he himself was unhurt.

Harry told me enthusiastically how effective the exercise of writing out his feelings and thoughts had been. It took only twenty minutes for Harry to rid himself of feelings that might have tortured him for days. He said, "It's frightening to think how ineffective I am when I haven't gotten rid of my negative feelings."

HER BOYFRIEND DIDN'T CALL

For Sarah, the most awful thing was her boyfriend not calling when she wanted him to. Boyfriends rarely call precisely when we want them to, so Sarah often felt hurt and frustrated. When Douglas did eventually call, she would react according to how hurt she felt. Of course, relationships don't easily survive this, and Doug decided to end it.

Things were no different with her next boyfriend, Russell. Sarah didn't know what to do. She couldn't get *any* of her boyfriends to call when she wanted them to. We all had to laugh when she told us her story, because there wasn't anyone at the seminar who hadn't had a similar experience. It's annoying when your lover doesn't call! Yes, we knew that Sarah could simply have called her boyfriend, but at the time she couldn't comfortably choose that solution.

Sarah suffered a lot of pain over quarrels about the issue. She didn't have the strength to 'go through' another boyfriend. She had finally met a man she was serious about, and wanted their relationship to last. She had managed to control herself and not give in to her anger, but she still felt annoyed about

Russell not doing exactly what she wanted when she expected him to. In general, Sarah experienced "feelings" as the most difficult and complicated part of her life, and we as a group understood exactly what she meant.

Sarah sighed with relief when we began doing the exercises. The idea of yelling into a tape while she waited for the expected telephone call appealed to her. This was something she could relate to. Her goal was completely clear: she would spew her venom onto the tape so that only her good side was left when Russell eventually did call. She hoped that this would prevent her from undermining their relationship. Sarah also learned how to feel her feelings and integrate them as soon as she felt them. Then she managed to listen to the information her feelings had to offer.

This story reminds me that looking at oneself in a more objective light has immediate benefits. Sarah later confided that she could well understand why boyfriend after boyfriend disappeared from her life. She had played back the tape and, hearing her venomous scolding, she realized that no man in his right mind would let himself be treated this way. It was a great relief to unburden herself of her feelings on the tape. Through this exercise, she learned to integrate her disappointment and anger and understand other people's reactions to them. She also learned to better respect Russell's right to call when he wanted to, rather than when she wanted him to.

FROM JEALOUSY TO MISUNDERSTANDING

Judy was newly married for the second time. She was very happy, but she hadn't counted on Scott's former wife, Susan, being part of the deal. While Judy had no children, Scott had a five-year-old son from his former marriage. Judy understood how important it was that Scott and Susan stay on good terms for the sake of their little boy, Sam. What made it tough for Judy was that she was jealous of Scott's relationship with Susan.

She felt it was childish to be jealous at forty-one, but she couldn't help herself, and the feeling persisted even after she and Scott married.

Judy wanted to stop being jealous so she could live peacefully with herself and Scott. She needed to find peace of mind, especially regarding Susan. All these feelings surfaced when she came to the seminar on self-management that a friend of hers had recommended.

After completing the seminar, Judy wrote out her painful feelings about Susan. Her state of mind lightened after each writing session, and though she found value in writing, as time went on she became somewhat bored. Judy knew that she hadn't gotten out everything about her jealousy, so she decided to try drawing her feelings, using huge sheets of paper and the thickest crayons. She drew a big, fat Susan on one side of the paper, enjoying every minute of making Susan ugly and shapeless, and was very cognizant of her feelings. On the other side she drew herself—as a great beauty!

Finally, Judy felt that her drawing exercise had done the trick. She felt light and quiet, and after awhile she was surprised to find herself thinking that the situation might not be so easy for Susan either. She shared her experiences with Scott, who was greatly relieved, and Judy realized how her feelings had blinded her. She understood that she'd been making Scott bear the burden of her jealousy. They talked for many hours, and made a real breakthrough in their relationship.

LIVING IS SHARING

Charles was the quiet type, and it had cost him dearly. He had kept to himself for most of his life, and had hardly released anything. When he turned fifty, life began getting unbearable. Everyone else at the seminar he was attending talked about him- or herself, but Charles didn't say a word, and his body language clearly revealed how introverted he was.

I asked him whether he wanted to talk with me. "Yes," he said. "Are you sure?" "Yes," he said again. It was hard to get more than a one-syllable response from Charles, but I could see that he really wanted to speak. During our talk, I just listened to *my* inner voice and let it give me the questions to help guide Charles.

Finally, a question touched something deep within him, sparking his need to share: "Aren't you longing to tell me what really happened, Charles?"

"I came home and found my wife in bed with another man."

The relief on his face when he opened up was evident. There were mostly men at this seminar, and they had each spoken about their problems and challenges. As they shared, an atmosphere of trust had developed among them. Other men have come home to find their wives in bed with another, but few wait twenty years to talk about their pain, as Charles did. As he began to speak, he had trouble and obviously felt uncomfortable, but as the words flowed, he regained his own voice. Charles had been "dead" in many ways during those twenty years, and he was taking an important step at the seminar.

In private, I suggested that he contact a psychologist who could help him better express his feelings. He agreed. "It's not easy for me to talk about myself. I think I'd rather go to my room and write now," he said when I asked him what his next step would be. He seemed relieved. Later, Charles told me that the process was slow, but he felt more alive and closer to other people. More importantly, he said that he was enjoying the journey into himself, and was learning to share himself more and more often as time went on. In short, Charles has become visible to himself and to others.

STORIES ABOUT CHILDREN

We grownups can help our children and other people's children when they have painful feelings. Irene Salvesen is a public school teacher who has kindly permitted me to share with you some of her classroom experiences. I think they might be helpful—at any age.

"I'm Going to Kill Him"

After lunch, Eli, a boy in the second grade, came back to class screaming, "I'm going to beat him, I'm going to kill him!" I hugged him and said, "You know you're not allowed to hit anyone or hurt anyone in any way here at school. But I see that you're angry, and there's nothing wrong with that. Would you like to draw or write something in the logbook?" (The children can write whatever they want in the logbook—things they are happy, or sad or angry about.) "Try to write out your anger, Eli."

"OK," he responded, "but I'm going to need every page in the book!"

Ten minutes later, he opened the door. "Come and see," he called with a big smile. On the first two pages of the logbook were a few rather gruesome drawings of his "enemy," Nils. On the next two were pictures of the fight they had had in the schoolyard, where Eli had been the stronger of the two. Finally, there was a drawing of Nils crying after Eli had hit him.

"Are you angry at me for drawing all these terrible things?" he asked.

"No, of course not! I told you that you could write anything you wanted as a substitute for hitting someone."

"I'm not angry at Nils anymore," Eli said, and went back to his seat and opened his math book.

The Teacher is a Witch

"It was a gray winter day, with sleet and rain. Walking to the last period with my first-grade class, I was met with quite a sight in the hall outside our classroom. Three boys and two girls were ladling water from a puddle outside the front door into the hall, using their boots as ladles! Instead of reprimanding them, I got some rags and a pail, and quietly told them to clean up, because they were responsible for the mess, not the janitor or me.

"Despite their loud protests, they got to work drying up the water. Ten minutes later the job was completed. One of the girls came up to me and said, "You were right to make us clean up, because we made all the mess." The others had an entirely different opinion. They were still furious at the unfair teacher, so I gave each of them a drawing pad and asked them to draw and write about why they were angry with me. They all did, and the pads were soon full of witches and monsters with my name on them. Suddenly, one of the boys tore his paper to pieces and went back to work with the rest of the class. He was obviously done being angry this time. The other boys followed suit immediately afterward.

"The one girl who remained just drew and drew, and wrote some, too. She had drawn a very ugly witch, with knives stuck into her heart and stomach and red tears running down her cheeks. 'You're clearly still very angry with me,' I said calmly. 'Yes!' she replied, but then began scribbling with a black crayon over everything she had drawn. She didn't stop until the whole page was completely black. And when the day was over, she gave me a goodbye hug as usual!"

NOBODY BELIEVED LITTLE ANDREW

Andrew was seven years old, and life was very hard for him. The problem was that his teacher didn't believe him when he said he was sick. She didn't let him call his mother at home. It was very painful for Andrew. Not being believed was almost as bad as being sick. His sister had been sick and in bed the week before, so he knew where he had caught his sickness. Luckily, Andrew had a wise father who took his problem seriously and was willing to listen to him when he came home. Andrew was deeply offended by his teacher, and he had a stomachache, a headache, and his leg hurt. It helped that his father sympathized with him.

When Andrew got up the next morning, he wasn't feeling perfect, but he wasn't very sick either. He was, however, very angry with his teacher. His father knew just what to do: he fetched a great big pillow and asked Andrew if he could pretend that the pillow was his teacher. Andrew had no trouble doing just that. Then his father asked him if he was angry with his teacher. "Yes! Really angry." Then he asked Andrew to repeat after him, "I'm so angry at my teacher," while hitting the pillow. Andrew yelled more loudly and more loudly and hit as hard as he could, until he no longer felt the need to yell or hit. Andrew had gotten rid of all his anger. After this exercise with his father he was free of any anger toward his teacher. He was even able to say how much he liked her.

Before leaving for school that day, Andrew whispered into his father's ear as he gave him a goodbye kiss. "Papa, I feel so much better!" It's important to have such a wise father, and it is good not to have to carry so much anger inside before the school day begins.

6

WHAT TO DO NEXT

—◆—

FINDING YOUR TALENTS

On a separate sheet of paper, write all the words that best describe your abilities. Don't limit yourself to the words on this list; add your own. Remember that your strength lies in what you like.

Reading / Analyzing / Operating / Managing / Giving orders / Discussing / Explaining / Preparing / Managing / Estimating / Finding / Learning by ear / Discussing / Clarifying / Taking part in / Cooperating / Writing / Deciding / Mediating / Translating / Marketing / Putting to use / Simplifying / Recruiting / Coordinating / Calculating / Choosing / Encouraging / Changing / Advising / Organizing / Predicting / Convincing / Evaluating / Putting together / Serving / Talking / Remembering / Ordering / Performing / Categorizing / Collecting / Acquiring / Selling / Creating / Mapping / Starting things / Classifying / Defining / Communicating / Recognizing / Researching / Demonstrating / Interviewing /

*Constructing / Localizing / Orienting / Drawing / Checking off /
Transferring / Matching / Being a part of / Questioning / Using /
Formulating / Reorganizing / Giving / Reporting / Identifying /
Revising / Budgeting / Selecting / Illustrating / Delegating /
Overseeing / Teaching / Bettering / Inspiring / Increasing /
Repairing / Playing with / Looking into / Deciding / Arranging /
Collecting information / Entertaining / Producing*

Discover Who You Are

On a separate piece of paper, write all the phrases that you
feel best describe you. Add your own phrases if you don't see
them here.

*I like details / I'm responsible / I enjoy playing / I like people
I work hard / I'm practical / I like to support others / I like
groups / I'm analytical / I'm stubborn, rigid / I'm well organized
/ I'm conservative / I like to control and dominate / I'm handy /
I'm independent / I like to make decisions / I'm an organizer /
I enjoy competition / I'm a dreamer / I like ideas / I'm lazy / I
like planning / I'm a spokesperson for change / I'm imaginative
/ I like to manage people / I never give up / I'm not particularly
sociable / I'm systematic / I like to take orders / I like to coordinate
/ I work with stability / I'm not self-reliant / I get right to the
point / I'm exacting / I have a creative mind / I'm verbal / I'm
technical / I like to motivate people / I'm artistic / I give up
easily / I like to give orders / I'm easily bored / I'm sociable*

Your Personal Inventory

After mapping your resources, try to express your abilities in words. Don't forget to write about the things you've achieved that gave you deep satisfaction. Your 'gemstones' are hidden in what you like doing most, what you're passionate about.

Base your job and your life on what you're truly impassioned about or you'll be just mediocre. Your passion will carry you onward to more meaning and success than you ever dreamed possible.

Give yourself plenty of time, and be honest with yourself!

Talents/Abilities:

Education:

Daydreams, deepest wishes:

Things you've done or achieved that have given you satisfaction:

What would you do if you had only one year left to live?

Write a clear description of your goal right at this moment:

EMOTIONAL INTELLIGENCE DEFINED

In 1990 Dr. John D. Mayer and Dr. Peter Salovey formulated the first scientific definition of Emotional Intelligence. In 1997, they published a revised, more cohesive definition: "The ability to perceive emotions, to access and generate emotions so as to assist thought, to understand emotions and emotional knowledge, and to reflectively regulate emotions so as to promote emotional and intellectual growth."

This book relies on their definition. What does it mean in leadership language? It means that to achieve the desired results, a good leader needs to be able to intentionally access, understand and manage his or her own emotions and the emotions of others. As a coach and leadership consultant, I've combined the academic research on EI with twenty years' applied consulting experience to create a working strategy for how to develop one's own EI. The four-fold division that follows is drawn from the most recent publications of Mayer and Salovey.

1. Identifying and Acknowledging Your Emotions and Those of Others

This is the ability to sense and identify feelings—the most important precondition for developing the other three elements of EI. Continually staying in touch with and examining your feelings is indispensable. A wide range of emotions— joy, sadness, fear, anger, love—is a sign of health. Sensing, feeling and being aware of your emotions is the most powerful tool for developing your EI. Your emotions are intelligent, and constantly give you important messages about yourself and the world around you.

Sensitivity to your own feelings is a precondition for being sensitive to other people's feelings and understanding their behavior. Emotions register in facial expression, tone of voice, and body language. Even people who consider themselves emotionally perceptive don't always read these messages correctly.

Empathy helps you identify with others and connect with them in ways that build meaningful social relationships. The ability to read people's signals of what they need and want allows you to share, work and play in more satisfying ways. Being able to feel what someone else is experiencing helps you understand things from their point of view—an invaluable ability for parents, teachers, leaders and salespeople. You live in a social world and constantly face the challenges of interrelating. Emotional intelligence enables you to meet the challenge. A high level of EI—well-developed emotional skills—results in great relationships, better team performance, and increased potential for advancement in the workplace. A low level of EI will hold you back.

2. Using Emotions to Facilitate Thought and Motivation

This means learning to integrate and channel your feelings so as to improve your thinking process and achieve the specific results you desire. This, too, requires constant awareness of your emotional state. Channeling your feelings liberates them, allowing you to express them openly and appropriately, as opposed to suppressing or losing control of them, which is destructive in the long run.

Paying attention to your feelings while you do something you love is actually using your feelings to generate motivation. Your feelings act as a "motor," energizing you; you're invincible when you tap into them. Your thoughts need the power of your emotions behind them to propel you forward. Nothing great was ever created without that power.

When you feel emotionally motivated, you can motivate other people, using your emotions to affect their thoughts and feelings. Charismatic leaders score high in the ability to use their feelings of motivation to inspire others. When you're brainstorming a new product or service, you want to project an upbeat mood that will rub off on your teammates, but in serious conversation with a customer, a more restrained feeling will be more effective. Even being negative is sometimes the emotionally intelligent thing to do. If you can channel your emotions, you'll be able to handle the unexpected, and manage critical situations using appropriate emotions to achieve the desired results. Being able to get people to feel what you feel is a characteristic of all great leaders.

3. Understanding Emotions: Going beyond acknowledgment, and deciphering the messages of feelings

In their article "Emotional Intelligence as Zeitgeist," Mayer and Salovey noted that in early Greek thought, the Stoic philosophers dismissed emotions as too subjective to merit attention. Fortunately, contemporary research reveals that our emotions convey significant, universal messages about social relations. What are your feelings trying to say to you? What are the deeper feelings hidden behind the more apparent ones? If you're in touch with your feelings, the answers to these important questions will surface. Your feelings are trying to tell you what's important to you. Their message is real and valuable. If you pretend not to feel what you're feeling, you'll lose information that you need to make better choices. It's well worthwhile to decipher your feelings; they're intelligent, and they always speak the truth about you. Feel them and analyze them, then ask yourself what you've learned that you can use to proceed in a more intelligent way.

4. Managing Emotions

Now we're talking about the ability to be aligned—to act according to your head and your heart. This is the highest branch of emotional intelligence, because it involves managing your own feelings and those of other people. It requires being able to focus your recognized strengths on a goal that you define, a goal you're passionate about, and directing your emotions and energy toward that goal. Your inner resources can trigger powerful emotions, which serve as catalysts for success. Self-motivation is a requisite for success, and relies on well-developed emotional awareness and acceptance.

In this context, leading and managing others by influencing their feelings depends on intentionally managing your own feelings. As a parent, teacher, business executive or other type of leader, you need to engender in a group the feelings you've first created in yourself. To foster creativity, you need to create an environment conducive to openness and trust, but first you have to create that environment in yourself. Similarly, when an environment of urgency, encouragement or motivation is needed, a leader has to create it within himself before transmitting it to others. While the appropriate response to a situation may vary, regulating emotions will help you implement an effective strategy for achieving the specific outcome you desire. Great leaders work at being able to recognize and manage their emotions intentionally and constructively, and cultivate the ability to understand and empathize with the emotions of others.

If you're not in touch with your emotions, you're not in control of your life: your feelings are controlling you. If you can't manage your emotions, you can't successfully manage, lead or inspire yourself and other people. We are here to give, not out of duty but because our hearts rejoice in giving. Emotional intelligence moves us to take action according to our inner voice. It's my strongest hope and dream that we will all want to choose to do some good, and to fulfill what is, ultimately, our shared mission: to leave the world a better place than we found it.

Randi B. Noyes

About the Author

Randi B. Noyes is a pioneer in the practical application of emotional intelligence and president of Leadership International, Inc., a leadership consulting firm. For over twenty years, Randi has provided leadership coaching to hundreds of top executives and corporate clients such as AT&T, Exxon, Mobil Oil and Phillips Petroleum.

After college, Randi left her native Norway to live in the United States. There she co-founded Scandinavia Inc., a successful ski apparel distributorship. In the course of business and during frequent transatlantic flights, Randi developed a passionate interest in understanding the forces that motivate people and lead to a successful, meaningful life. After realizing that many people she talked with started their own businesses or improved their careers, Randi left the sportswear business to focus on self-leadership and team building. In 1979 she founded Business Presentation Inc., a leadership consulting firm.

In 1995 Randi published the Norwegian edition of *The Art of Leading Yourself: Tap the Power of Your Emotional Intelligence.* It became a bestseller in Scandinavia and made her a sought-after speaker. In June 2000, Leadership International hosted a senior leadership conference with Dr. John Mayer, the originator of the first scientific definition of emotional intelligence. In 2002, *The Art of Leading Yourself* won the Business Book of the Year Award from *Foreword Magazine.*

Randi offers results-oriented consultations to executives and corporations in all industries. Based in Boston, Massachusetts and Oslo, Norway, she can be reached at:

www.leadership-international.com.

Also available from Vermilion

CONFIDENCE IN JUST SEVEN DAYS
Practical strategies to transform your life
Ros Taylor, Dr Sandra Scott and Roy Leighton

Lacking in confidence? Here's how to get it in just seven days!

Some people are just plain shy, but even the seemingly most confident and successful people find certain areas of their life difficult to negotiate. In *Confidence in Just Seven Days*, three experts offer their most effective techniques for conquering shyness – in just seven days.

LIFE MAPPING
Create a powerful blueprint to bring out the best in yourself – and your life
Brian and Sangeeta Mayne

The complete approach to creating balance and harmony in your life.

Life Mapping is a unique personal empowerment technique designed to help you identify your life purpose and be the most magnificent 'you' that you can be. Simple to understand and fun to use, *Life Mapping* is both profound in its depth and great in its rewards.

THE SECRETS OF HAPPINESS
100 Ways to True Fulfilment
Ben Renshaw

Full of witty and practical tips, and written in a positive, uplifting style, this delightful book brings succinct advice on finding fulfilment and peace of mind from Britain's answer to John Gray.

WHO MOVED MY CHEESE?
An amazing way to deal with change in your work and in your life
Dr Spencer Johnson

Over 12 million copies sold!

What began as a 94-page self-help book has grown into a major international bestseller. Written for all ages, this story takes less than an hour to read, but its insights last for a lifetime. The book is the work of MD turned management guru Dr Spencer Johnson, whose *One Minute Manager* sold more than 7 million copies.

The message is simple – 'change isn't everything, it's the only thing. Embrace change; don't fight it.'

'One of the most successful business books ever' *Daily Telegraph*

☐	Confidence in Just Seven Days	0091856655	£7.99
☐	Life Mapping	0091884551	£8.99
☐	The Secrets of Happiness	0091887542	£4.99
☐	Who Moved my Cheese?		
	(paperback)	0091816971	£5.99
	(hardback)	0091883768	£10.99

FREE POSTAGE AND PACKING

Overseas customers allow £2.00 per paperback

BY PHONE: 01624 677237

BY POST: Random House Books
C/o Bookpost, PO Box 29, Douglas
Isle of Man, IM99 1BQ

BY FAX: 01624 670923

BY EMAIL: bookshop@enterprise.net

Cheques (payable to Bookpost) and credit cards accepted

Prices and availability subject to change without notice.
Allow 28 days for delivery.
When placing your order, please mention if you do not wish
to receive any additional information.

www.randomhouse.co.uk